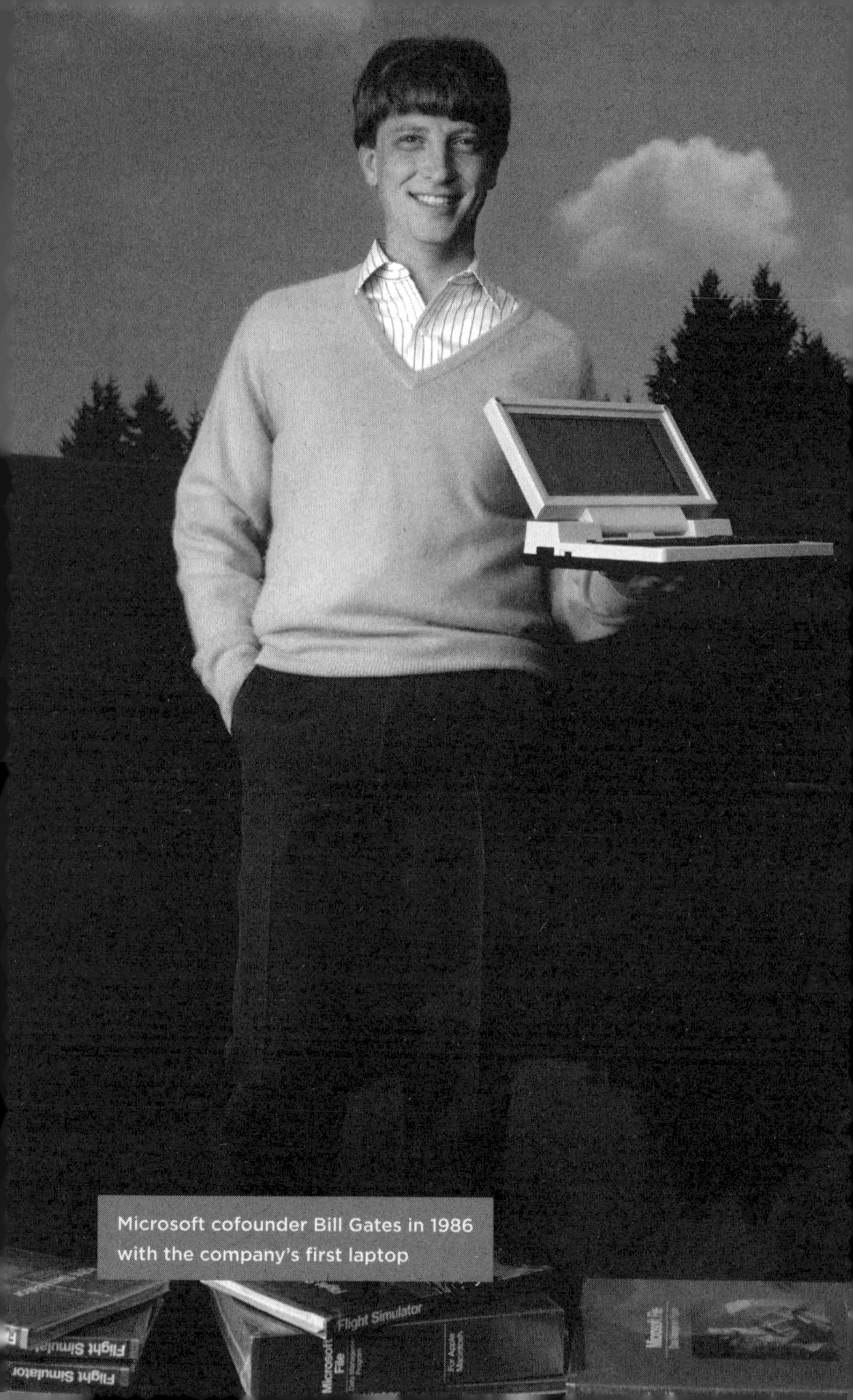

Microsoft cofounder Bill Gates in 1986 with the company's first laptop

MICROSOFT

CREATIVE COMPANIES

SARA GILBERT AND NELL MUSOLF

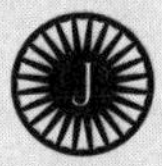

JAICO PUBLISHING HOUSE

Ahmedabad Bangalore Chennai
Delhi Hyderabad Kolkata Mumbai

Published by Jaico Publishing House
A-2 Jash Chambers, 7-A Sir Phirozshah Mehta Road
Fort, Mumbai - 400 001
jaicopub@jaicobooks.com
www.jaicobooks.com

Published in arrangement with
The Creative Company
2140 Howard Drive West,
North Mankato, MN 56003, USA

Design by Graham Morgan
Art direction by Tom Morgan
Edited by Jill Kalz

Images by Alamy (artpartner-images.com, Dave Jepson, Ian Shaw), Getty (Bettmann, Chris Ratcliffe/Bloomberg, Christian Petersen, David Ryder/Bloomberg, Doug Wilson, Jaap Arriens/NurPhoto, James Leynse, Joe McNally, Rick Maiman, Ron Wurzer, STAN HONDA/AFP, Thiago Prudencio/SOPA Images), Pexels (Ekaterina Bolovtsova, Nothing Ahead, Pixabay, Salvatore De Lellis), Unsplash (Kote Puerto), Wikimedia Commons (Brian Smale and Microsoft, Bruce Burgess, Enterely, Jelson25, Jesús Gorriti, LPS.1, Marcin Wichary, Miles Harris, United States Department of Justice (DOJ))

MICROSOFT
ISBN 978-93-49358-46-1

First Jaico Impression: 2025

Printed by
Parksons Graphics Pvt. Ltd., Mumbai

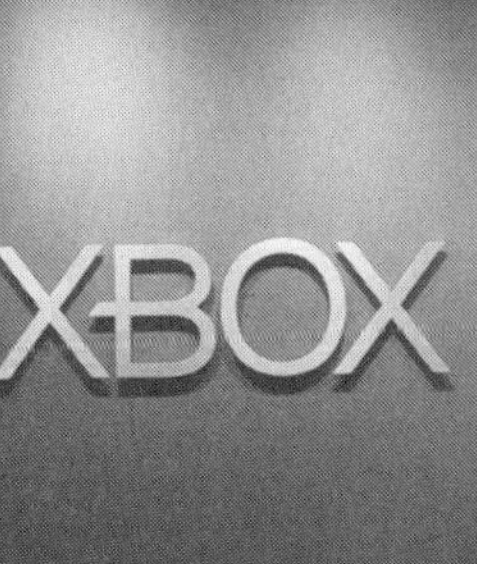

Inside the Microsoft campus in Redmond, Washington

The Windows keyboard key is multifunctional.

CONTENTS

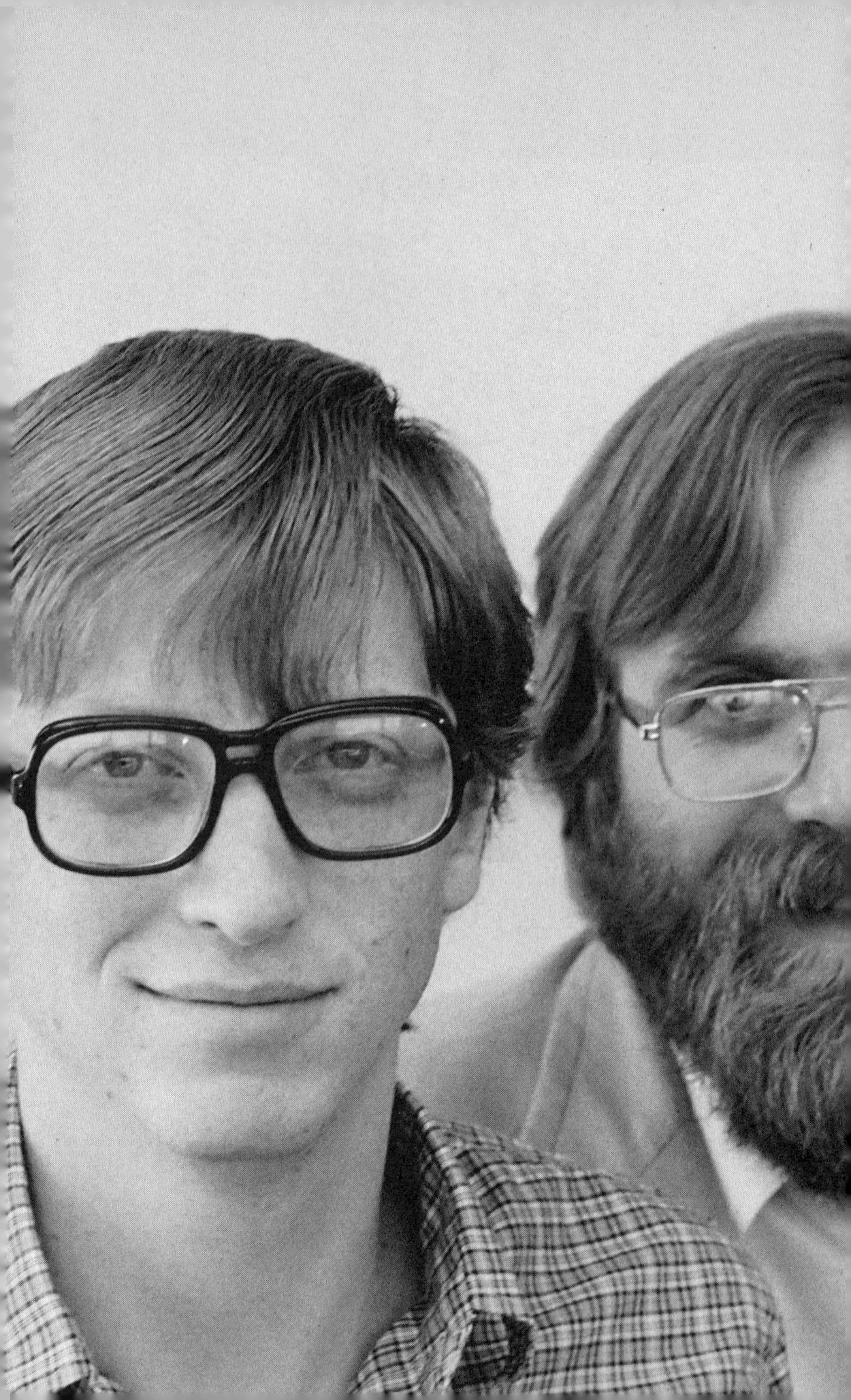

Introduction

It started with strings of **code** being written by hand on yellow legal pads in a dorm room at Harvard University in Cambridge, Massachusetts. Stopping only to eat pizza and take sporadic naps, and with the help of a few classmates, Bill Gates and Paul Allen wrote their first programming language in just eight weeks.

OPPOSITE: Shown here in 1983, Bill Gates (*left*) and Paul Allen (*right*) were friends with a shared passion for computer science.

Almost 40 years later, the same frenzied pace still powers the company that Gates and Allen started: Microsoft. But now, the programmers have the highest tech computers at their fingertips. They have espresso machines to help keep them awake and a full-service cafeteria available to satisfy their hunger. They have walking trails on which they can stretch their legs after sitting for too long. And their coding projects encompass not just programming languages but video games, cloud computing, **artificial intelligence** (AI), and more.

The goal of changing the world with technology, however, is still the same. It's what has fueled Microsoft from its very earliest days.

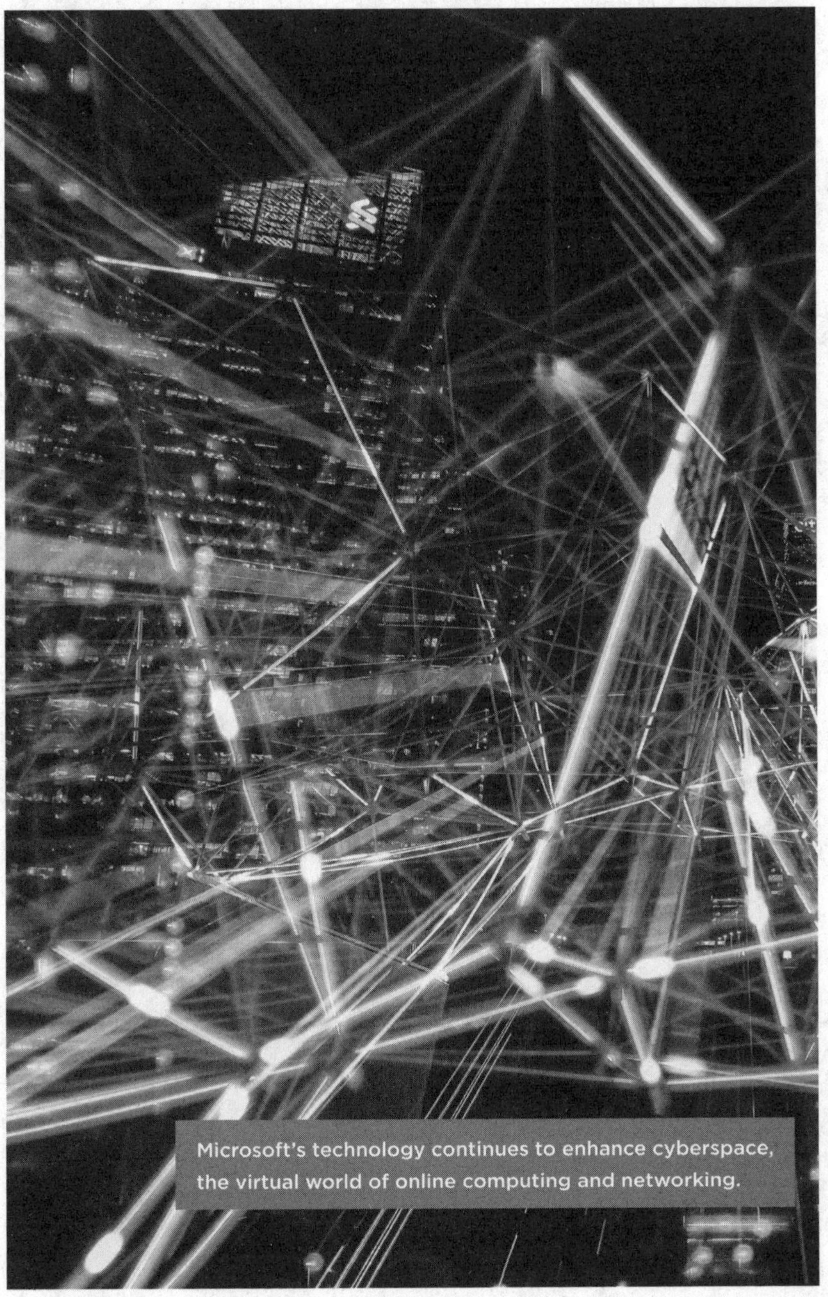

Microsoft's technology continues to enhance cyberspace, the virtual world of online computing and networking.

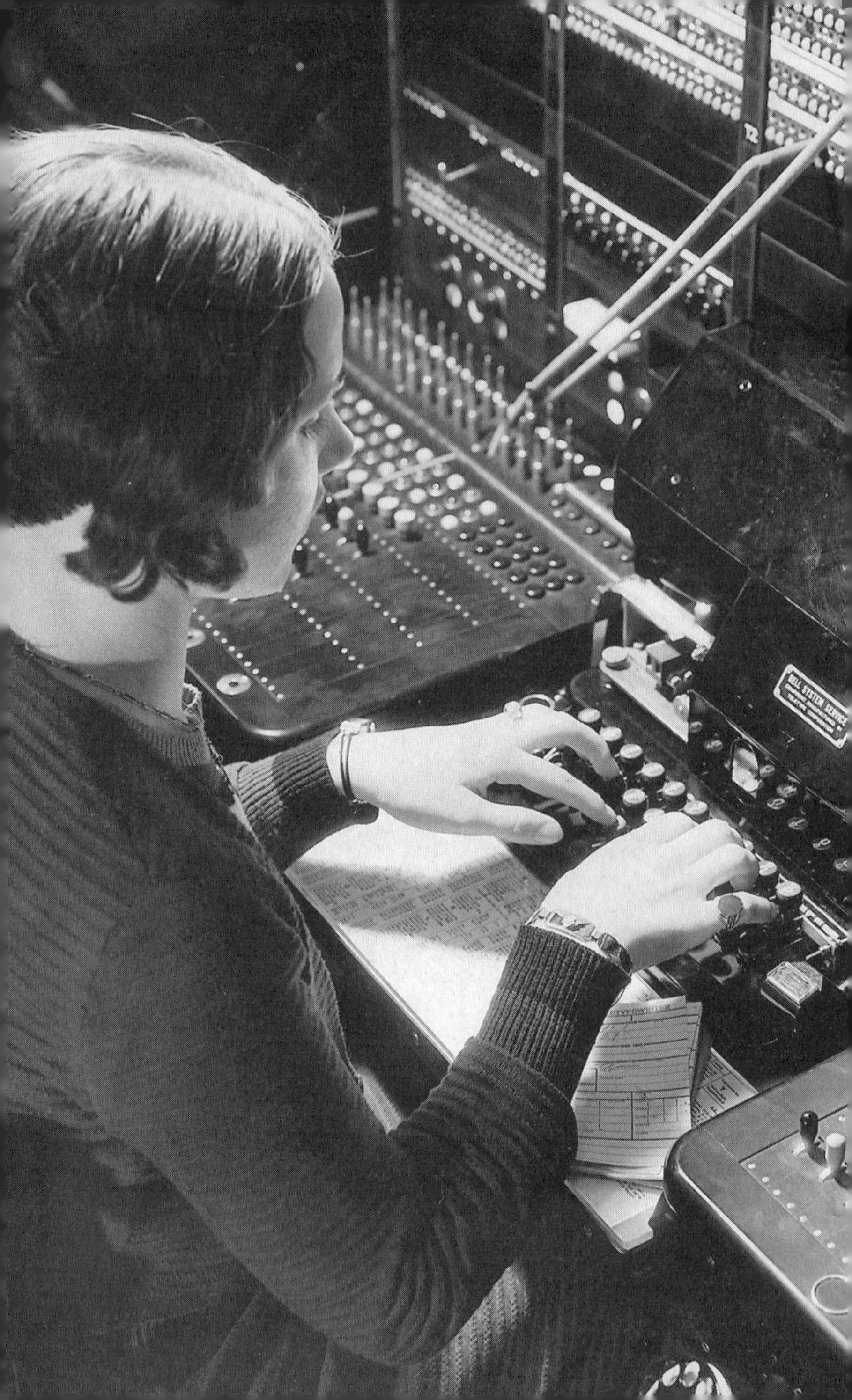
BELL SYSTEM SERVICE

Beginning with BASIC

There weren't computers in all the classrooms at Lakeside School, the all-boys private middle and high school in Seattle, Washington, that Bill Gates attended in the late 1960s. At that time, computers were still quite large, bulky, and expensive. But the teachers at the school could see that computing was going to be important soon.

OPPOSITE: The Teletype electronic typewriter of the early 1900s (and its ability to send messages electronically) fascinated Bill Gates.

Several of the Lakeside teachers worked together to buy one very early computer terminal for the school. That terminal fascinated Gates and several of his classmates. They were so intrigued by the emerging technology that they started the Lakeside Programmers Club. It was a student group devoted to writing computer programs.

Gates and his friends—including Paul Allen, who was a few years older—learned enough about programming to develop a payroll system for a local business and computerize their school's class schedules. They speculated about what else could be possible once computers were more common. "Don't you think that someday, everybody will have one of these things?" Gates asked Allen at one point. "And if they did, couldn't you deliver magazines and newspapers and stuff through them?"

Allen graduated from Lakeside in 1971. He earned a perfect score of 1600 on the SAT, a college admissions standardized test, and enrolled at Washington State University to study computer science. Gates graduated two years later, having fallen just short of Allen's perfect SAT score with a 1590. He went to Harvard University as a pre-law major but loaded his schedule with math and computer science classes. By that time, Allen had already quit college. He had started working for Honeywell, an electronics company based near Boston, Massachusetts. The two friends were in close proximity again.

In December 1974, when Allen saw a story calling the Altair 8800 the world's "first minicomputer" in *Popular Electronics* magazine, he took a copy over to Gates's dorm room at Harvard. That sparked a conversation about how these new computers were going to need more software—programs that run the computer and tell the **hardware** what to do. Gates and Allen decided that they were going to help create that software.

The two friends reached out to the owner of Micro Instrumentation and Telemetry Systems (MITS), the company that created the Altair 8800. They told him that they had created a computer language based on a 1960s general-purpose programming language known as BASIC, which stands for Beginner's All-Purpose Symbolic Instruction Code. Their program, they explained, would allow the Altair 8800 to inter-

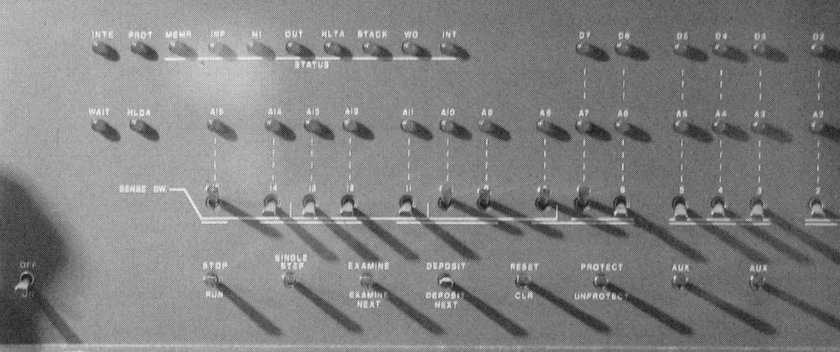

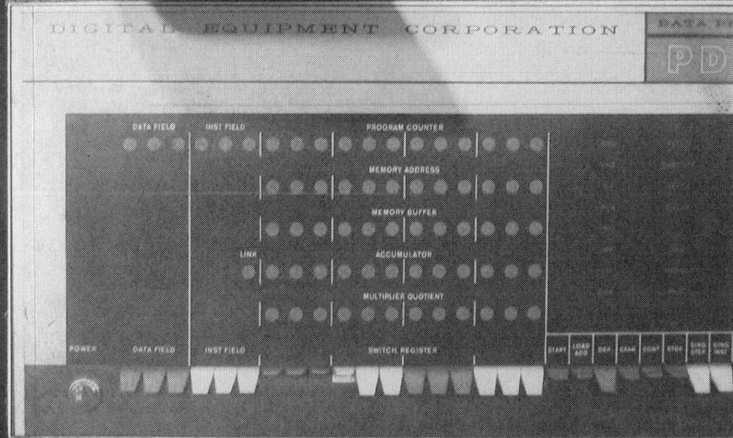

The Altair 8800 offered Gates and Allen a chance to create their own computer language.

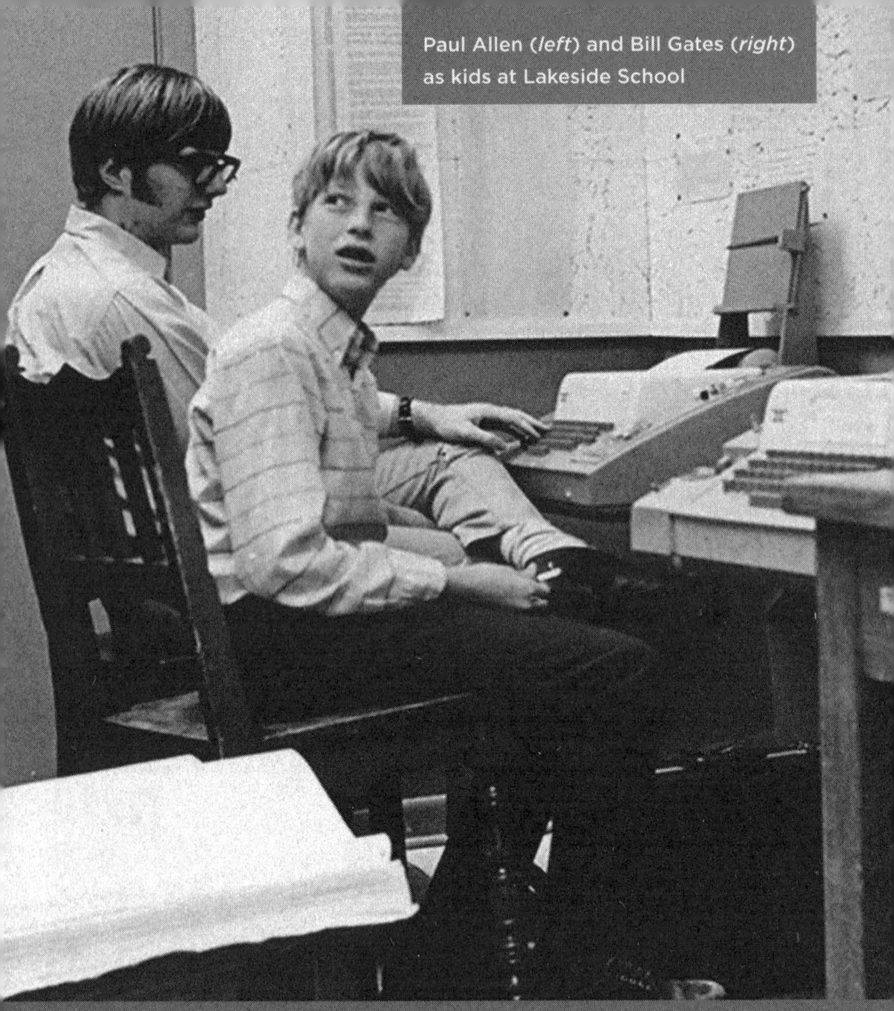

Paul Allen (*left*) and Bill Gates (*right*) as kids at Lakeside School

Paying for Computer Time

Very few schools had computers in 1968. But thanks to $3,000 raised by a group of mothers at a rummage sale, Lakeside School in Seattle, Washington, was able to lease time on a Teletype Model 30 computer. The lease allowed Lakeside's students, including Bill Gates and Paul Allen, to have limited access to the computer. The two friends spent as much time as possible learning how to use it and quickly became experts. Gates returned to his high school to give a graduation speech in 2005. "If there had been no Lakeside, there would have been no Microsoft," he told the students.

pret BASIC and make it easy to use the computers. Ed Roberts, the owner, was intrigued and wanted to meet with the men to learn more. He told them that he had heard from several other programmers and that the first to show up at his office would have the best shot at a contract with the company.

In truth, Gates and Allen hadn't written their version of BASIC yet. Now, motivated by the challenge to get to MITS first, they had to hurry. They worked around the clock during Gates's Christmas break and through January to finish it. In February 1975, Allen flew to Albuquerque, New Mexico, to present Altair BASIC to Roberts.

Roberts quickly saw that Altair BASIC was efficient and easy to use. He offered Gates and Allen a contract—and Allen a job as the company's vice president of software. Allen left Honeywell and moved to Albuquerque to work with MITS. Gates stayed at Harvard to finish his sophomore year but joined Allen in New Mexico over the summer. While he was there, the pair decided to start a software company of their own. They named it Micro-Soft, a combination of the words *microcomputing* and *software*. Before the end of the summer, they had dropped the hyphen and called their company Microsoft.

Gates stayed in Albuquerque that fall to work with Allen before returning to Harvard for the spring semester of his junior year. He stayed until the end of the following fall semester,

TAKEAWAY

The pair decided to start a software company of their own. They named it Micro-Soft, a combination of the words *microcomputing* and *software*.

but he was more interested in working on software with Allen than in completing his degree at Harvard. In 1976, he dropped out and moved to New Mexico to devote his time entirely to Microsoft.

It was good timing. Another pair of young **entrepreneurs** named Steve Jobs and Steve Wozniak had just started building computers in a garage in Palo Alto, California. In 1977, they introduced the Apple II personal computer, which had an **operating system** that worked best for playing games. When users complained that they wanted more, Microsoft offered to sell a new version of

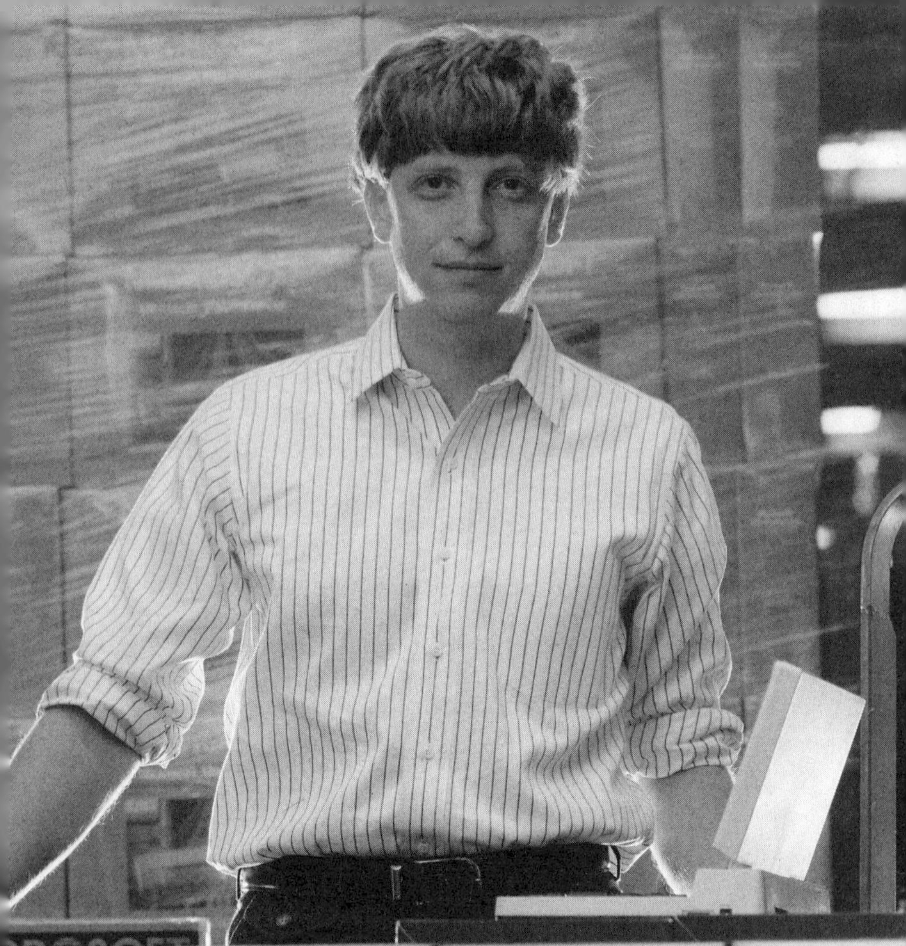

From Dropout to Doctoral Degree

Bill Gates never earned a college degree. He enrolled at Harvard as a math major in 1974 but dropped out to help build Microsoft with Paul Allen. In 2007, Harvard invited him back and awarded him an honorary Doctor of Laws degree. "We recognize the most illustrious member of the Harvard College class of 1977 never to have graduated from Harvard," Provost Steven Hyman said. Gates started his speech with a message to his dad, who had traveled to Cambridge, Massachusetts, for the ceremony. "Dad, I always told you I'd come back and get my degree," he said.

BASIC—Applesoft BASIC—to the company for $31,000. Applesoft BASIC was installed on the more than one million Apple II computers that were sold in the late 1970s.

By then, Microsoft's relationship with MITS had grown uncomfortable. MITS wanted sole use of the BASIC languages, but Microsoft wanted to be able to sell them to other computer companies. Gates and Allen could already see that there would be a growing market for computer languages and did not want to be restricted to one client. On April 20, 1977, they sent Roberts a letter terminating their licensing agreement with MITS. Once the details of the split were settled, they made another decision: to move Microsoft, including the 12 employees now working for the company, to their hometown of Seattle.

```
if ( message
{
    // Need to let
    ErrorLogfile.log (
    sessionManager.
    addTORXCache ( 
    setSequenceState (
}
else if ( fix.protocol.
{
    // Just forward Sequence
    forwardMessage ( message );

    Cache ( message, cur
    State ( RECOVERI
```

Operating at Full Strength

Microsoft started 1979 in an office on the eighth floor of the Old Bank Building in downtown Bellevue, a suburb of Seattle. The company was still focused on software, but Gates and Allen knew it was time to move beyond BASIC languages. The staff had more than doubled, but everyone, aside from a single secretary, was tasked with programming.

OPPOSITE: From the way things look onscreen to the way programs function, everything on a computer starts with lines of code.

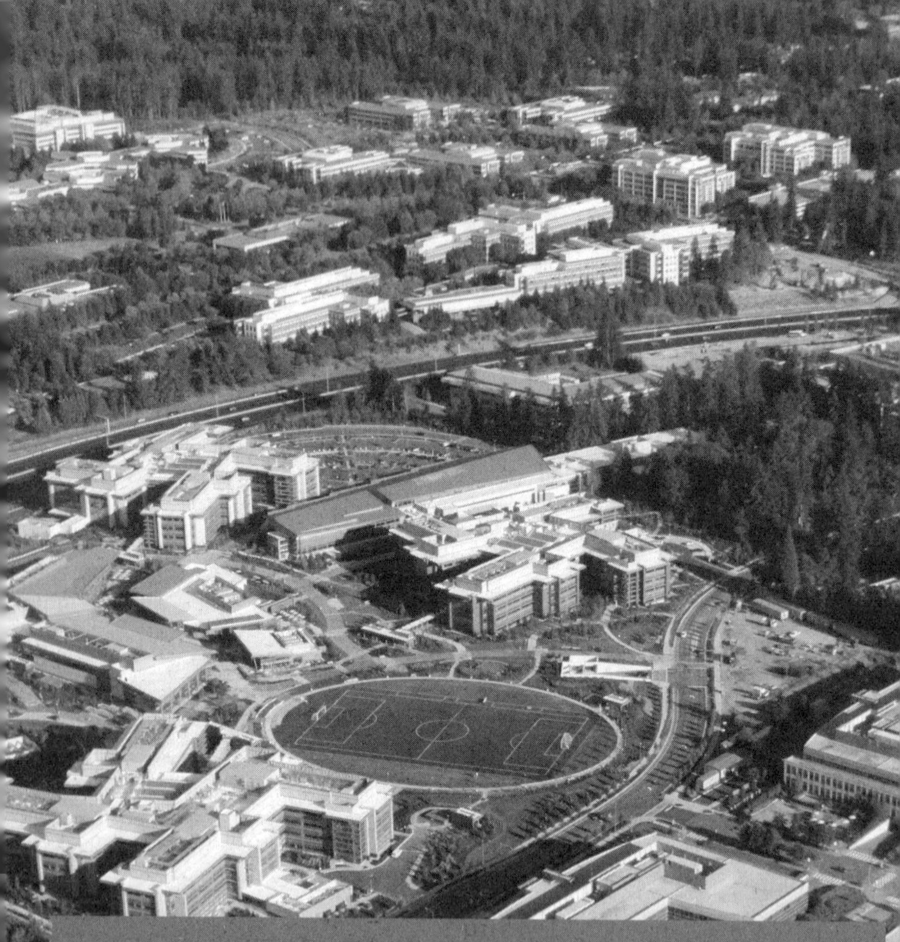

The Microsoft Campus

In 1986, Microsoft moved its headquarters to a 30-acre (12-hectare) lot in Redmond, Washington. The campus started with six office buildings. They were built around a pond that came to be known as "Lake Bill," because cofounder Bill Gates could see it from his office. Since then, the campus has expanded significantly. It now encompasses 130 buildings with more than 20 million square feet (1.9 million square meters) of office space on more than 500 acres (202 hectares) of land. More than 50,000 people work there—which makes it larger than some small cities! Although some of the original six buildings have been replaced, Lake Bill remains untouched.

To grow the business, Microsoft not only needed to bring in more developers and programmers but also technical writers and administrative staff.

One of those hires was Steve Ballmer, one of Gates's former classmates at Harvard. Ballmer, who had lived down the hall from Gates, had graduated in 1977 with degrees in applied mathematics and economics. He had started working toward his master's degree in business administration at the Stanford Graduate School of Business when Gates lured him away to join Microsoft. He joined the team as first assistant to

Gates, who was now the president of Microsoft. Ballmer's expertise was in business, not in computers. He took over many of the administrative duties, freeing Gates up to work on development.

Ballmer's business savvy came in quite handy when Gates and Allen were developing a relationship with International Business Machines Company (IBM). IBM was creating a new line of personal computers and asked Microsoft to create the operating system that would allow the computer to use various programs. Ballmer helped Gates and Allen purchase an existing language

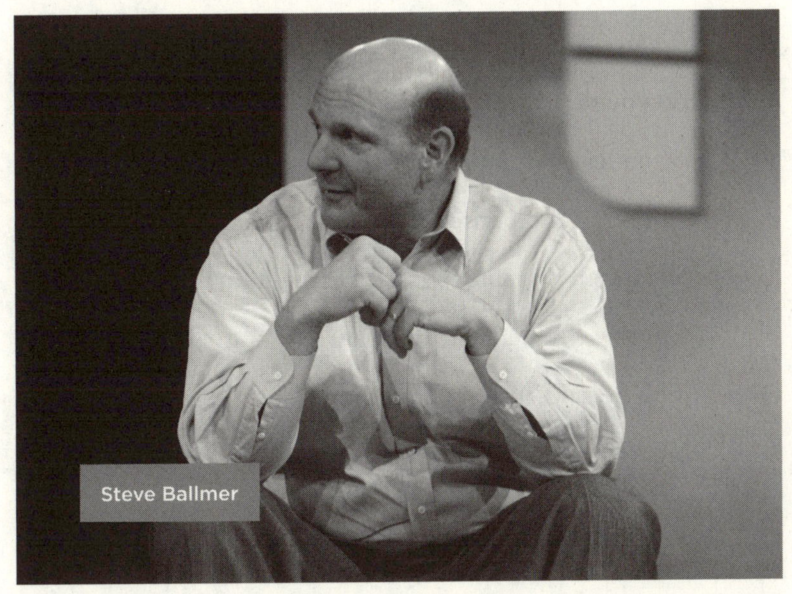
Steve Ballmer

called Q-DOS from Seattle Computer Products, a small tech company, which they used to create MS-DOS (Microsoft Disk Operating System). MS-DOS was released with the IBM PC in 1981.

MS-DOS quickly became the operating system for manufacturers of personal computers, including Commodore and Tandy. As the number of computers sold soared in the early 1980s, so did Microsoft's

revenues. In 1982, Microsoft brought in annual revenues of $24.5 million. But as the company was growing, its expenses did, too. Ballmer had insisted on bringing in more top talent to the company, which Gates was reluctant to do. "You're trying to bankrupt me," he said, although he eventually agreed to the hires if the company's revenues also grew.

In 1983, cofounder Paul Allen's resignation rocked the company. Allen's relationship with Gates had grown strained over the years. The two argued frequently. When Allen was diagnosed with Hodgkin's disease, he made the decision to leave Microsoft. "To be 30 years old and have that kind of shock—to face your own mortality—makes you feel like you should do some of the things that you haven't done," Allen said. After successful medical treatment, Allen remained on the **board of directors**

TAKEAWAY

In 1983, cofounder Paul Allen's resignation rocked the company. Allen's relationship with Gates had grown strained over the years. The two argued frequently.

at Microsoft but never returned to daily operations. Instead, he chose to devote his time to other interests beyond computers, such as sailing and various **philanthropic** endeavors.

As Allen was wrapping up his time at Microsoft, Steve Jobs was ramping up production of a new Apple computer: the Macintosh. Jobs wanted Microsoft to develop software programs for the "Mac," as it was known. Gates directed his staff to develop a graphical user interface

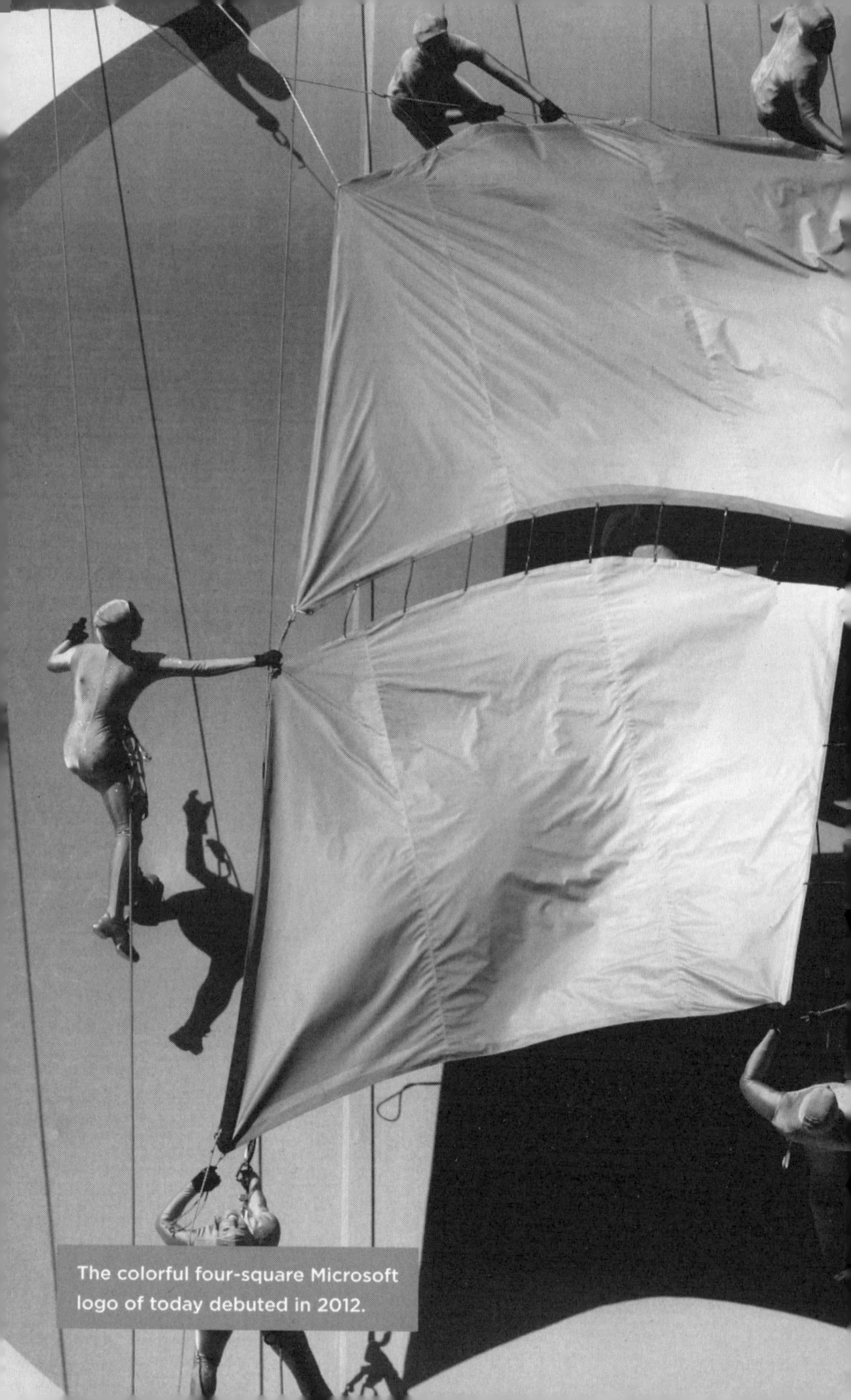

The colorful four-square Microsoft logo of today debuted in 2012.

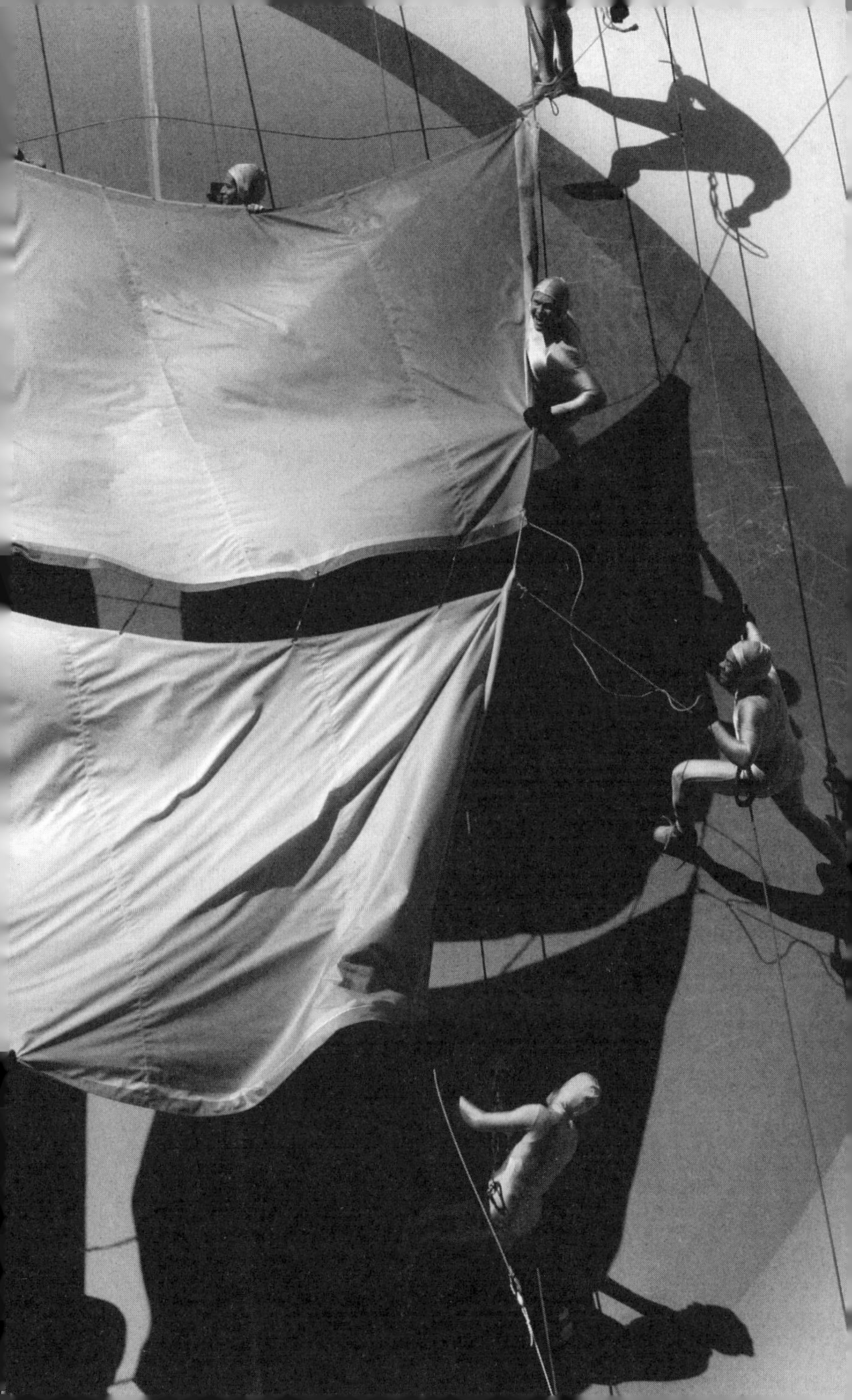

(GUI) that could be used on both Apples and IBM-compatible computers, knowing that Microsoft would benefit more from serving both major players in the market.

But there were other developments in the works that would prove even more profitable for Microsoft. Late in 1983, the company introduced Microsoft Word. The advanced word-processing program could be used with the MS-DOS operating system and, eventually, on Macintosh computers, as well. In 1985, the first version of Microsoft Windows was released.

TAKEAWAY

Windows was a revolutionary product. It allowed MS-DOS users to open multiple "windows" that displayed the contents of folders and files without having to type commands.

Windows was a revolutionary product. It allowed MS-DOS users to open multiple "windows" that displayed the contents of folders and files without having to type commands. Instead, they could use a click of their "mouse." This new handheld computer accessory allowed users to control a cursor on screen to point and click on files, folders, and other icons. But as innovative as Windows was, it had significant problems that frustrated users. For example, although multiple windows could be open at a time, they couldn't overlap one another on the screen. Open windows also used a great deal of memory, which caused computers to crash.

As Microsoft programmers went back to work on improving Windows, the now 10-year-old company started thinking about becoming a publicly traded company. The decision would allow people outside the company to buy **stock** and become part owners of Microsoft. On March 13, 1986, not even one month after Microsoft had

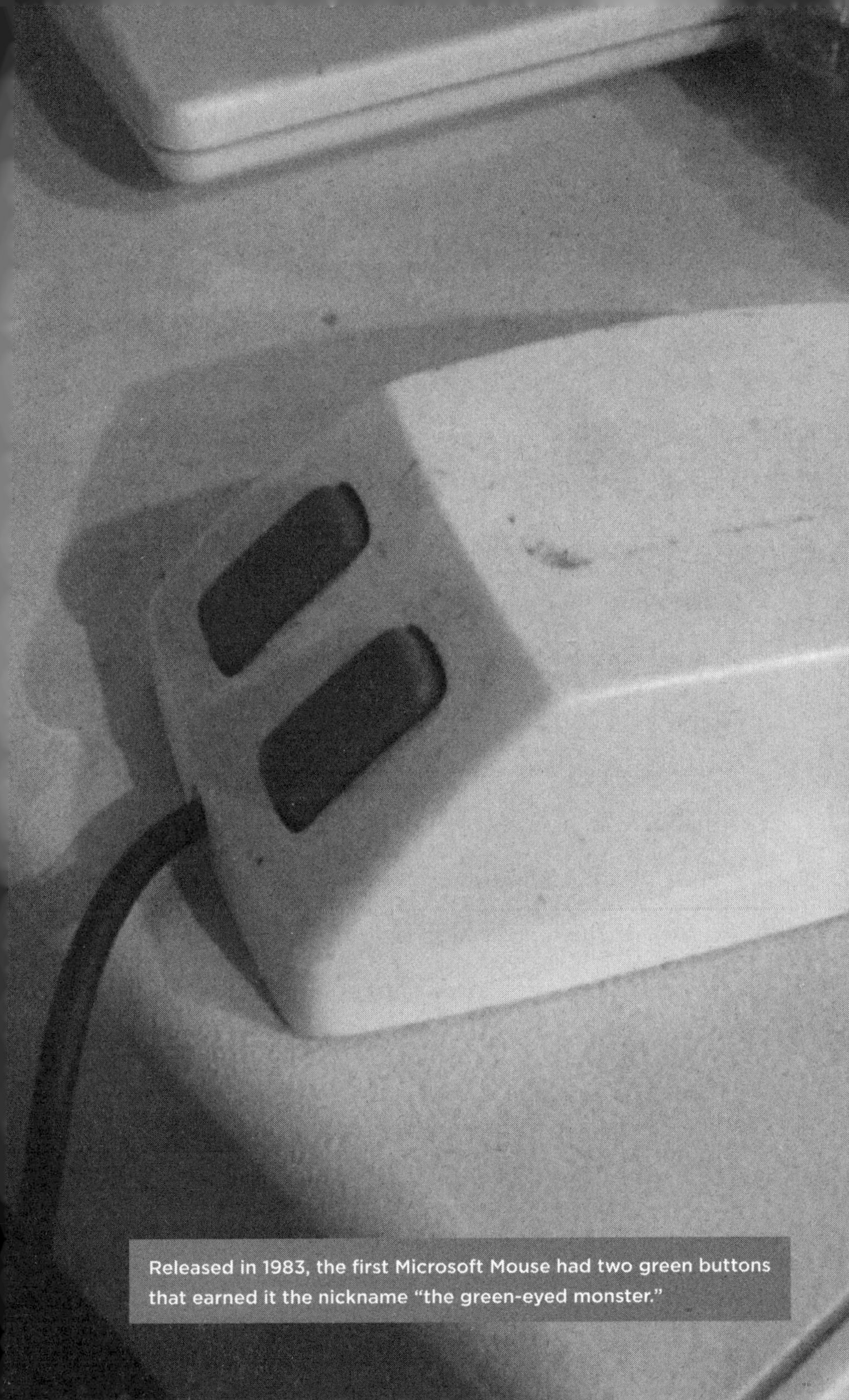

Released in 1983, the first Microsoft Mouse had two green buttons that earned it the nickname "the green-eyed monster."

moved to its new location in Redmond, Washington, approximately 2.5 million shares in the company were sold, raising $61 million. Gates owned 45 percent of the company, which was worth $350 million at the time.

That value would soon skyrocket—but before that could happen, Microsoft was plagued by battles surrounding its ongoing work on Windows. Apple filed a pair of lawsuits. It claimed that the idea for Windows came from Apple's design and that certain aspects of Windows copied aspects of Apple's design (Microsoft eventually won both cases). At the same time, Microsoft's relationship with IBM was on the rocks. The updated Windows 2.0 was outselling its OS/2 product—which had also been designed by Microsoft. IBM contended that Microsoft had put less effort into the design

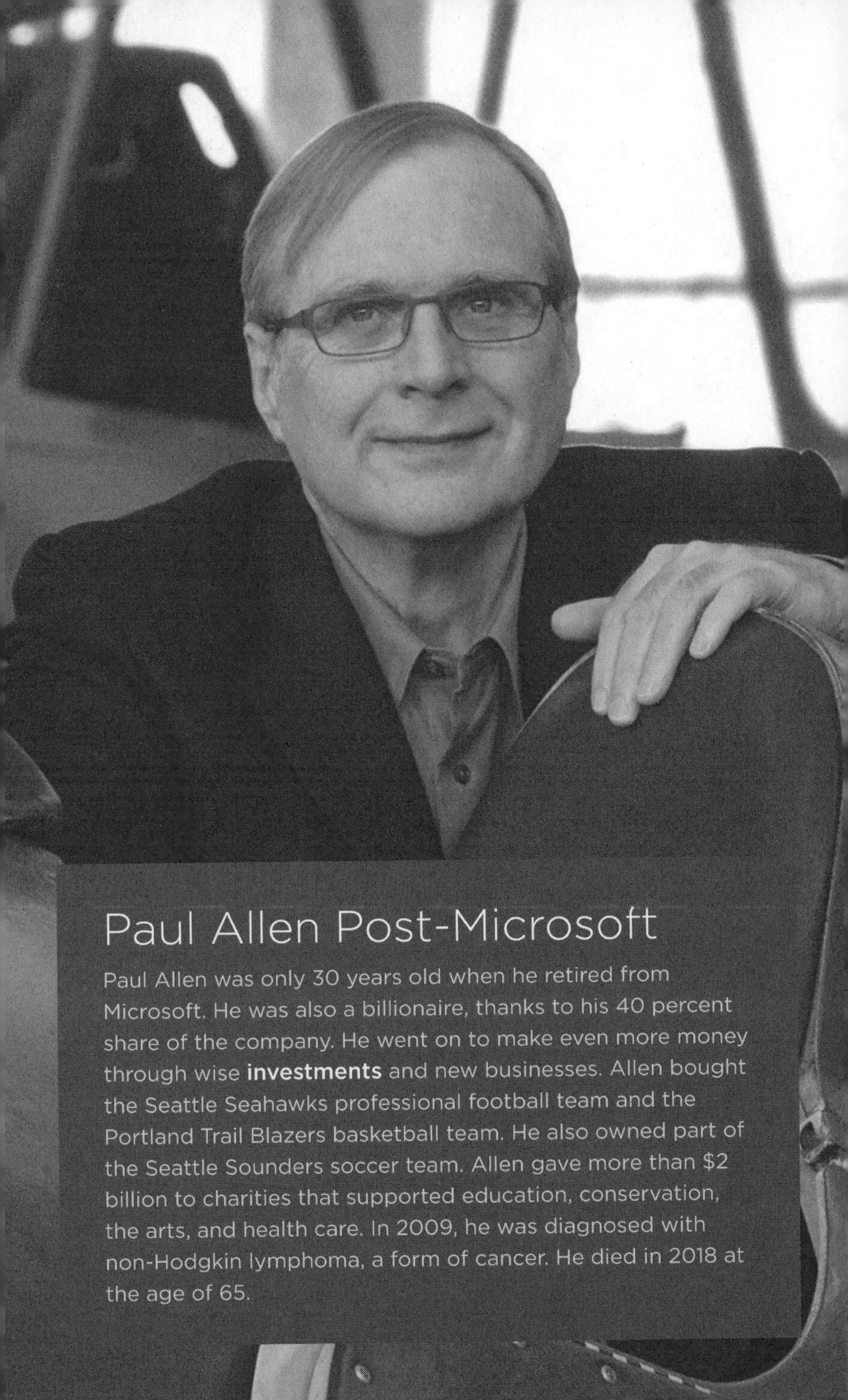

Paul Allen Post-Microsoft

Paul Allen was only 30 years old when he retired from Microsoft. He was also a billionaire, thanks to his 40 percent share of the company. He went on to make even more money through wise **investments** and new businesses. Allen bought the Seattle Seahawks professional football team and the Portland Trail Blazers basketball team. He also owned part of the Seattle Sounders soccer team. Allen gave more than $2 billion to charities that supported education, conservation, the arts, and health care. In 2009, he was diagnosed with non-Hodgkin lymphoma, a form of cancer. He died in 2018 at the age of 65.

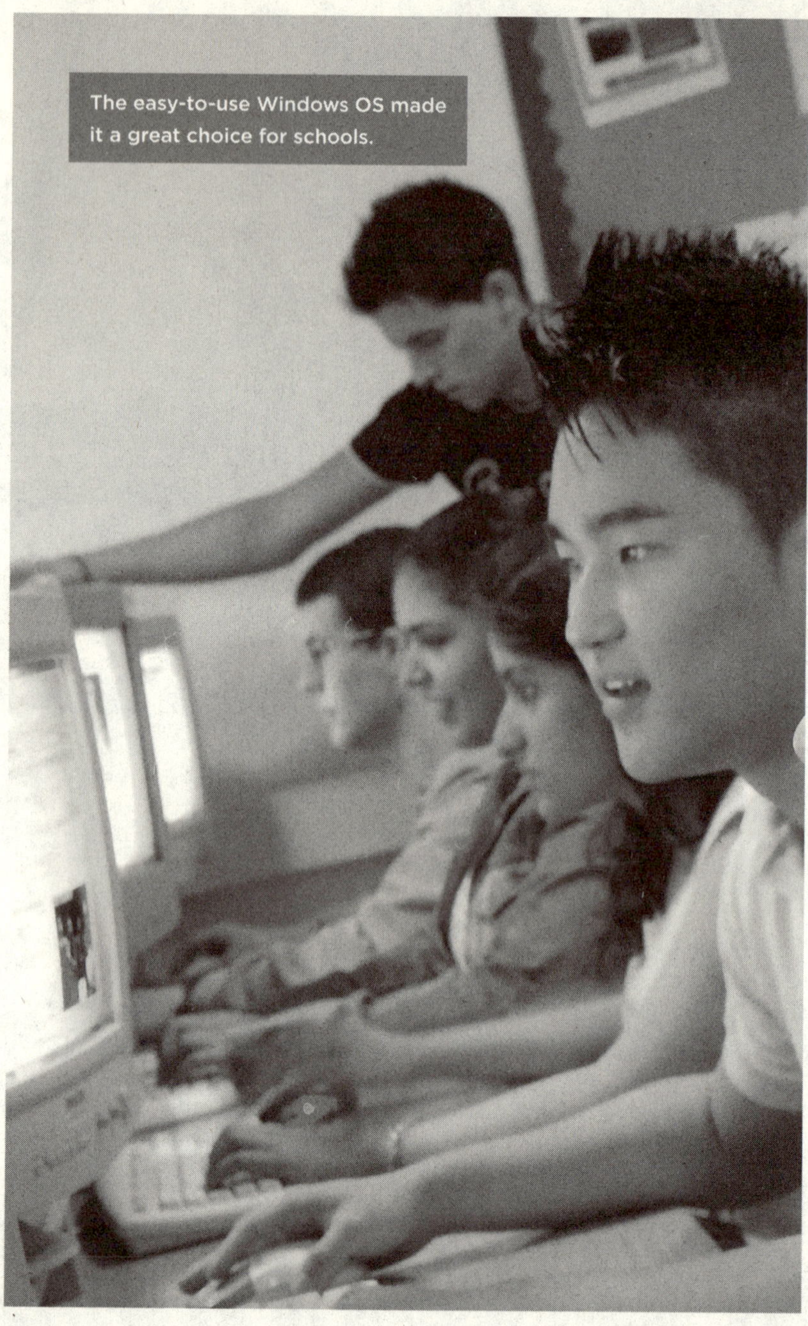

The easy-to-use Windows OS made it a great choice for schools.

of OS/2 intentionally so that it couldn't compete with Windows.

Then, in 1990, Microsoft launched Windows 3.0. Finally, the company had gotten it right. The redesign included better memory support and a more colorful user interface, which customers appreciated. Positive reviews, paired with a massive, $10 million **marketing** campaign, led to more than 100,000 copies being sold during its first two weeks on the market and helped Microsoft top $1 billion in sales that year. By 1993, more than one million copies of Windows 3.0 and its subsequent iterations were selling each month. And almost 90 percent of the personal computers being used in the world ran on a Microsoft operating system.

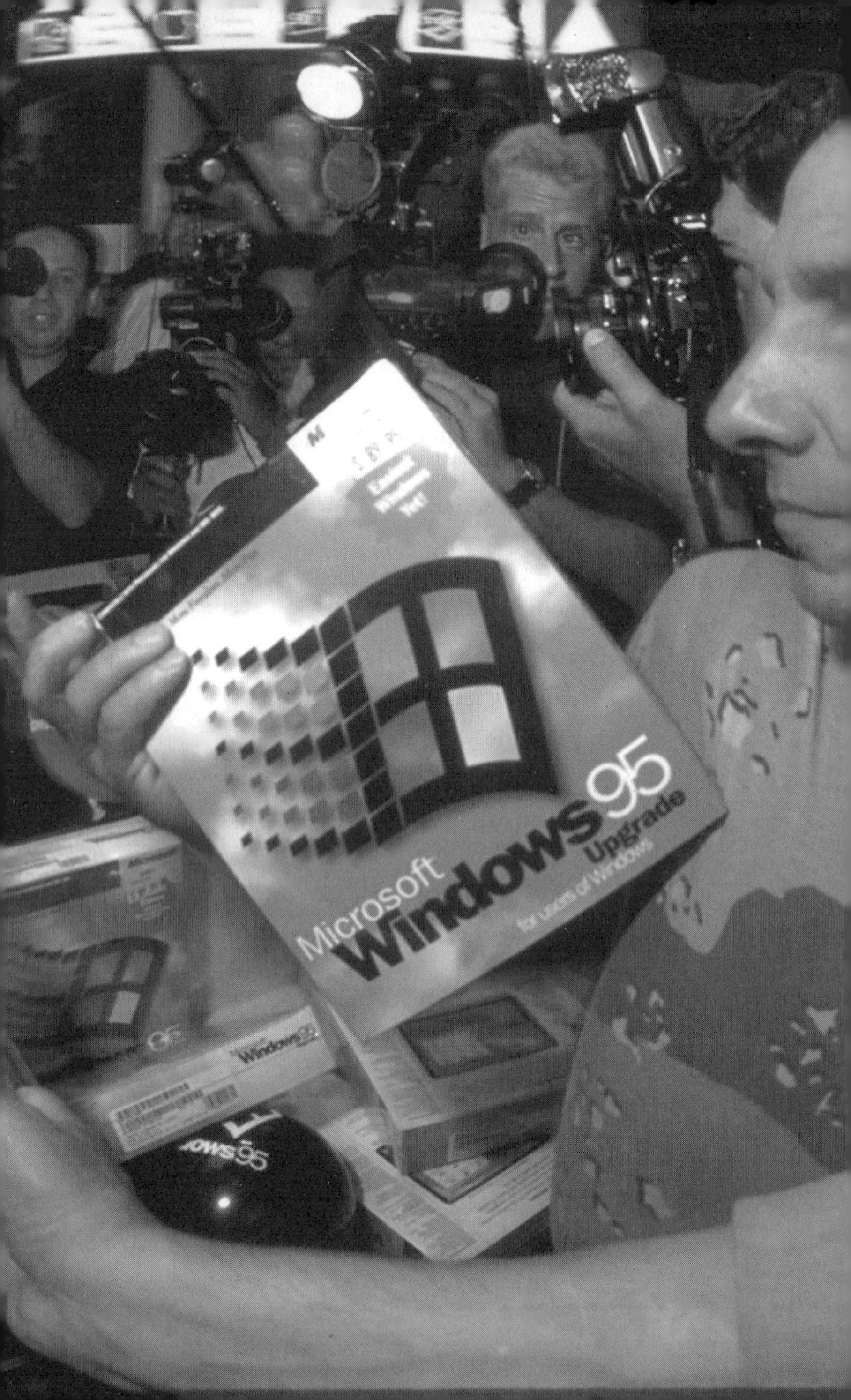
Microsoft
Windows 95
Upgrade
for users of Windows
Windows 95

Long Lines and Lawsuits

At midnight on August 24, 1995, computer stores around the world opened their doors to lines of shoppers, all waiting to buy the same thing: Windows 95. It was Microsoft's newest software package that had been hyped for weeks. The company had spent $150 million promoting the launch, which included the creation of a video guide starring Jennifer Aniston and Matthew Perry from the television show *Friends*.

OPPOSITE: More than one million copies of Windows 95 were sold in North America within the first four days on the market, with the rest of the world following suit.

It also spent $12 million for the rights to use the song "Start Me Up" by the Rolling Stones. One of the most anticipated features of the new operating system was the "Start" button.

The investment paid off: Users worldwide loved Windows 95 and snapped up seven million copies within the first five weeks of its release.

Microsoft, which had been in business for 20 years by that time, had more than 16,000 employees and was turning a **profit** every year. In 1995, when it also launched Microsoft Network, a full-service Internet provider,

Changing the World

The technological **innovations** that Bill Gates led through Microsoft have impacted the world, but the foundation he started with his former wife may be even more impactful. Since its founding in 2000, the Bill and Melinda Gates Foundation has contributed more than $53 billion to help make the world a healthier place. The foundation works with partners in more than 130 countries to help improve health care, eliminate poverty, and improve the lives of children. It has also expanded to fund advancements related to AI. Even after Bill and Melinda Gates divorced in 2021, their work through the foundation continued.

and MSNBC, a 24-hour television news channel, profits eclipsed $1.4 billion. But that success brought with it resentment from competitors. Some of them insisted that Microsoft's ever-present operating system was breaking laws protecting fair competition. In 1994, Microsoft changed some of its sales practices in response to an investigation by the U.S. Department of Justice. But the outcome wasn't quite as simple a few years later, when the company faced one of the biggest lawsuits in the history of U.S. business.

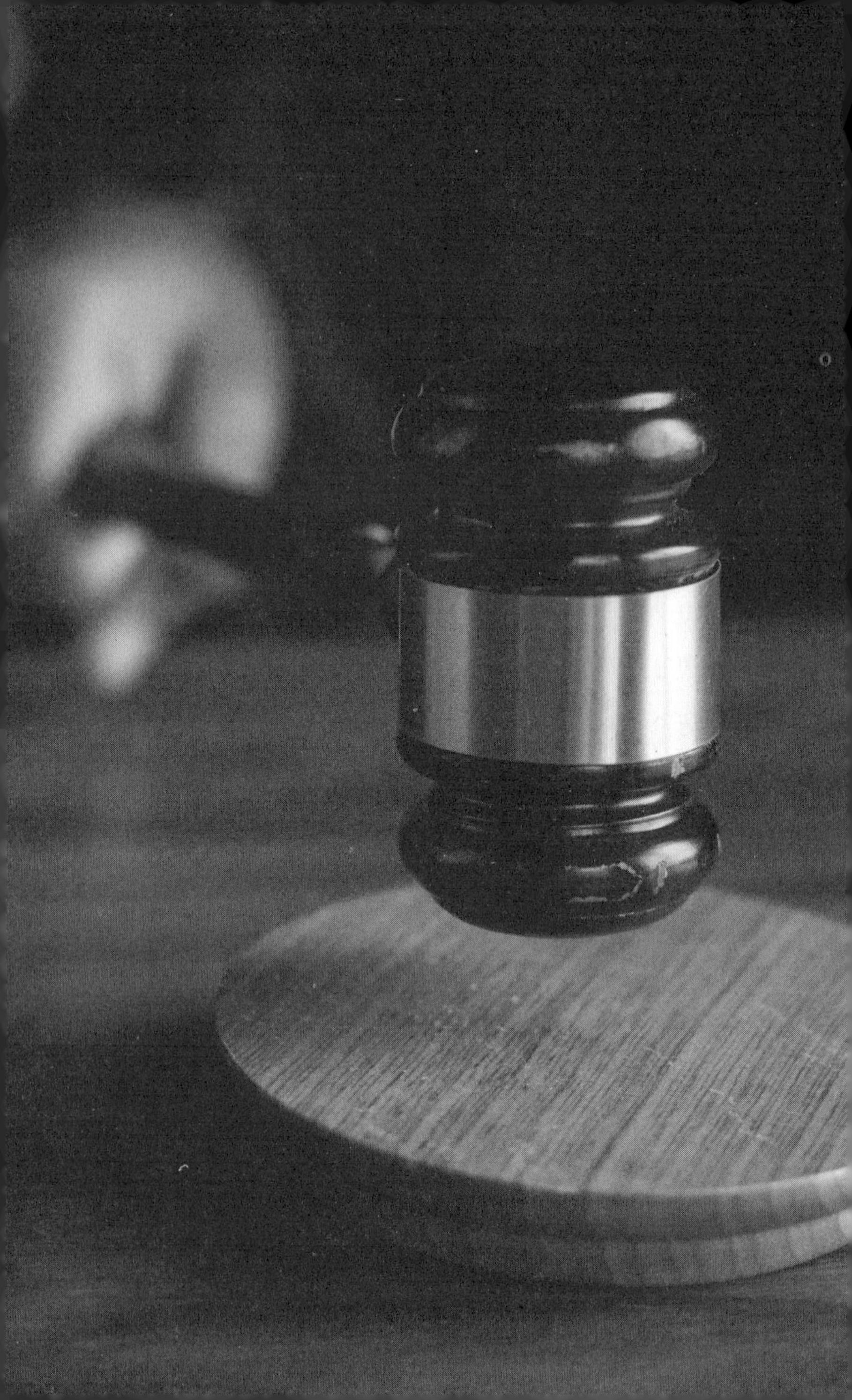

The lawsuit came about when the U.S. Department of Justice alleged that Microsoft had broken **antitrust** laws by bundling its Windows 98 operating system with its Microsoft Internet Explorer browser. Doing so, the lawsuit said, was an attempt to force other browser companies—such as Netscape and America Online (AOL)—out of the market. Those smaller companies couldn't compete in the Internet browser space because Microsoft's operating system was sold with so many computers. The Justice Department claimed that Microsoft was close to having a **monopoly.** It recommended that the company include other browser options in its software packages. That proposed solution was not popular among Microsoft

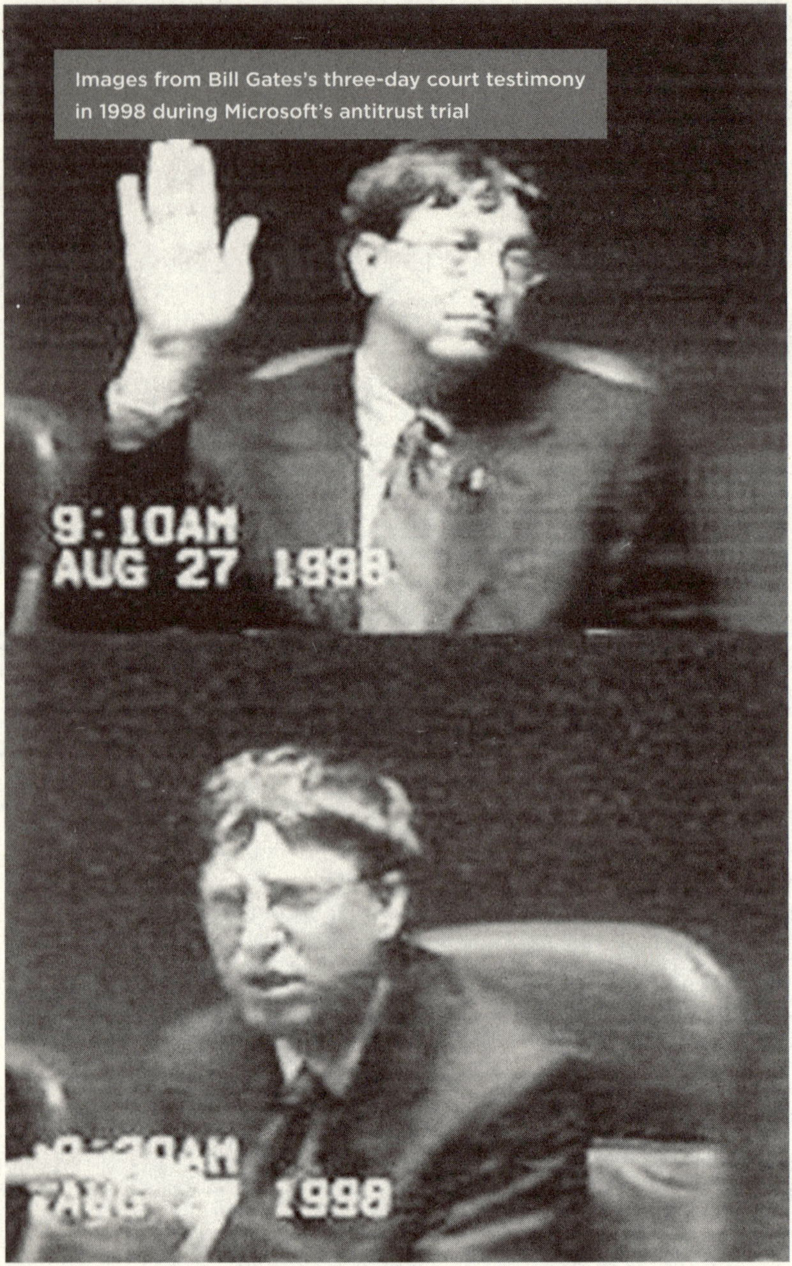

Images from Bill Gates's three-day court testimony in 1998 during Microsoft's antitrust trial

executives. "It would be like asking Coca-Cola to ship three Pepsis with every six-pack," one remarked after hearing the government's idea.

In 1999, after a marathon trial that lasted 30 months, a judge ruled that Microsoft had violated antitrust laws. The ruling ordered the company to be broken up so that it couldn't control the marketplace so completely. Microsoft **appealed** the ruling. Although the appeals court maintained that Microsoft was guilty of trying to build a monopoly, it overturned the order to break it up. But there were conditions: Microsoft had to allow three independent monitors to work at its campus and provide them with full access to the company's records and personnel for the next five years. It also had to provide other software makers with information that would allow them to develop programs that were as compatible with the Windows operating systems as Microsoft's own products. Microsoft also agreed to donate software, computers, and training to more than 12,500 schools.

Amid the legal challenges, Bill Gates stepped down as the chief executive officer (CEO) in 2000 and promoted Steve Ballmer to the role. Although Gates retained his position as chairman of Microsoft's board of directors and became the company's chief software engineer, he wanted to focus more time on the philanthropic foundation that he and his wife, Melinda, had started. Ballmer's

Gaming Gold

While Microsoft was developing its Xbox gaming console, Bungie Studios was developing a fantasy military strategy game called *Halo*. In 2000, before either the game or the Xbox had launched, Microsoft bought Bungie Studios so it could publish and distribute *Halo*. *Halo* became one of the most popular video game series of all time. It racked up more than $6 billion in sales over its 20-year span. It also helped propel the popularity of the Xbox. When Bungie Studios separated from Microsoft in 2007, Microsoft established a new division called 343 Industries to continue producing games for the series.

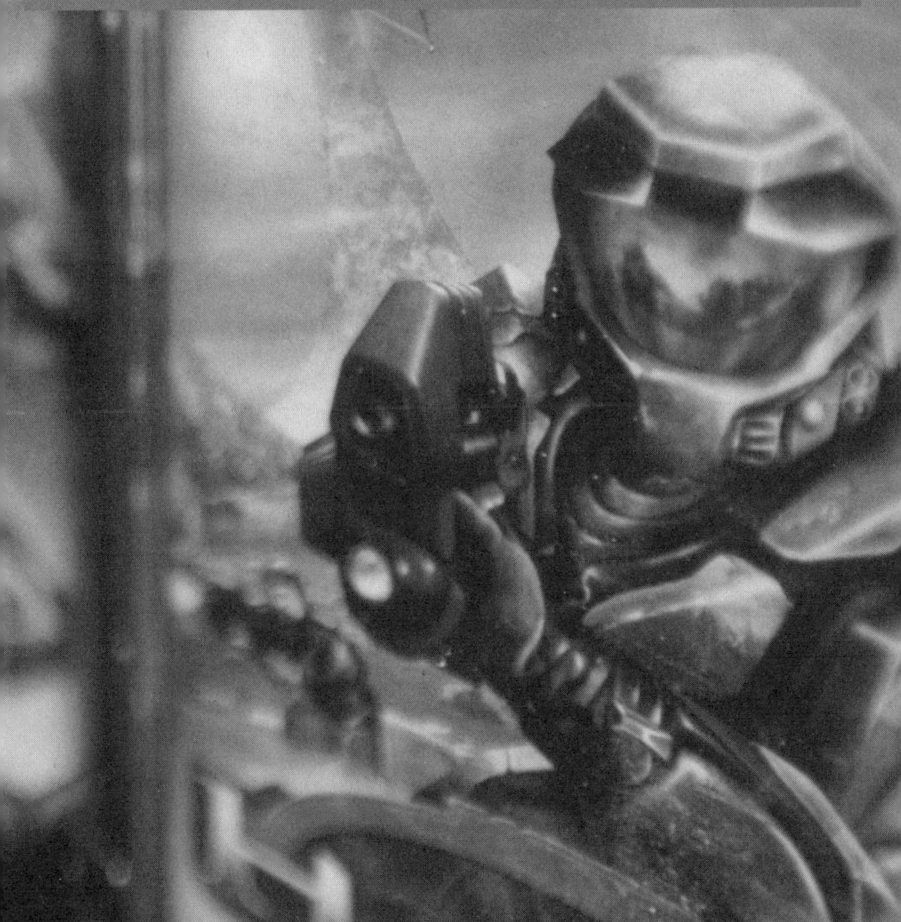

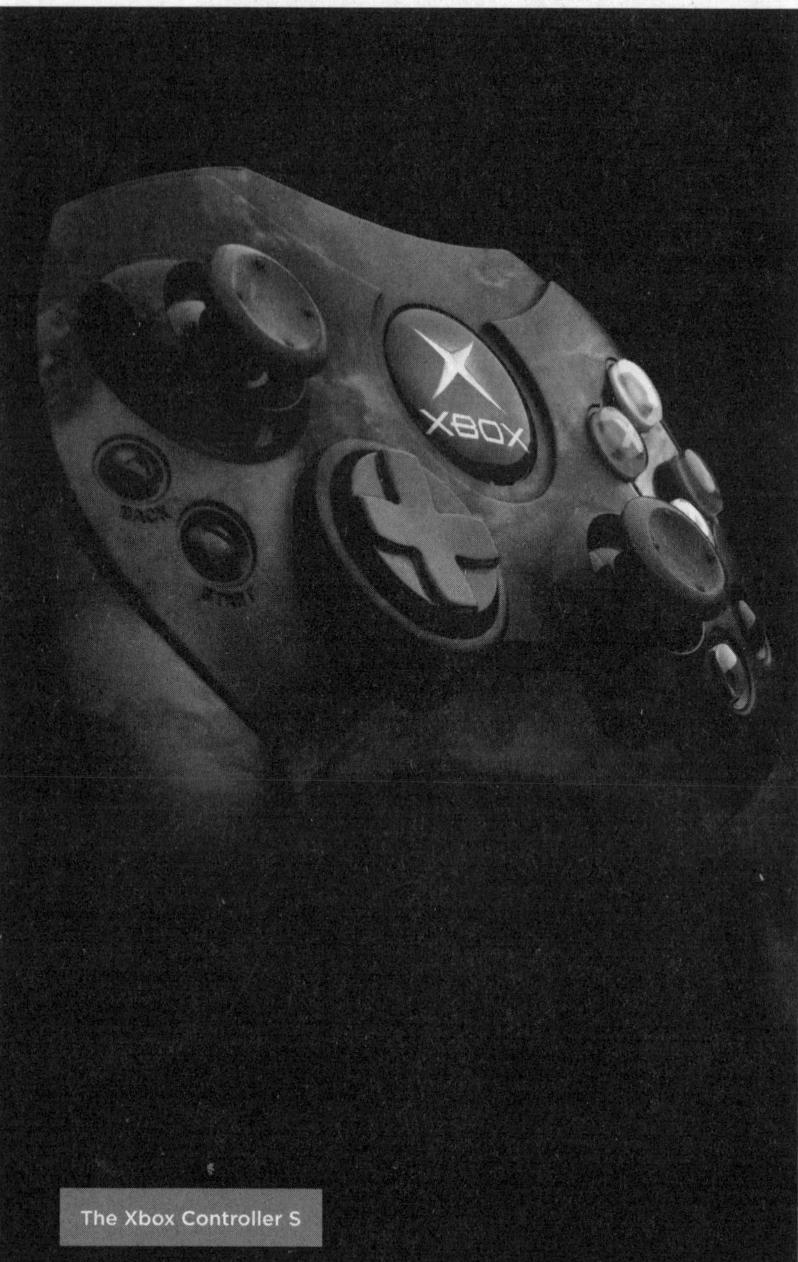

The Xbox Controller S

plan was to continue building the company around the next generation of Windows as well as software geared around the Internet.

One of the first new initiatives under Ballmer's leadership was the 2001 introduction of the Xbox, an electronic gaming console that opened a whole new product category for the company. Sony was the leader in gaming systems, and the Xbox had been designed to compete with its PlayStation. Microsoft continued developing the Xbox, introducing Xbox Live, an online gaming experience, in 2002 and releasing the more powerful Xbox 360 in 2005.

Although the Xbox was well received by gamers, the PlayStation remained more popular. The introduction of Nintendo's Wii console in 2006 created even more competition. Microsoft eventually cut the price of its system to gain more market share. By 2010, the Xbox 360 was the most used game console in U.S. homes.

Gaming wasn't the only area in which Microsoft was seeing increased competition. Google had launched its successful **search engine** in 1998. Apple had moved into mobile devices with its iPods in 2001 and iPhones

TAKEAWAY

By 2010, the Xbox 360 was the most used game console in U.S. homes.

in 2007. In 2009, Microsoft introduced Bing, a more robust successor to its MSN search. It was described as a "decision engine." It not only provided search results but also empowered users to make intelligent decisions based on what was found. In 2010, Microsoft announced its first Windows Phone. Both new products struggled against the established leaders, putting Microsoft in the unfamiliar position of underdog.

By the time Microsoft celebrated its 30th anniversary in 2010, it was operating without either of its founders involved in day-to-day operations. Paul Allen had left the board of directors and sold most of his stake in the company in 2000. Bill Gates remained chairman of the board, but he had stepped away from playing an active role in 2008. The value of the company's stock had been flat for several years. Microsoft was ready for new leaders to help propel the company in a new direction.

The Windows Phone struggled for years to compete, until finally being discontinued in 2019.

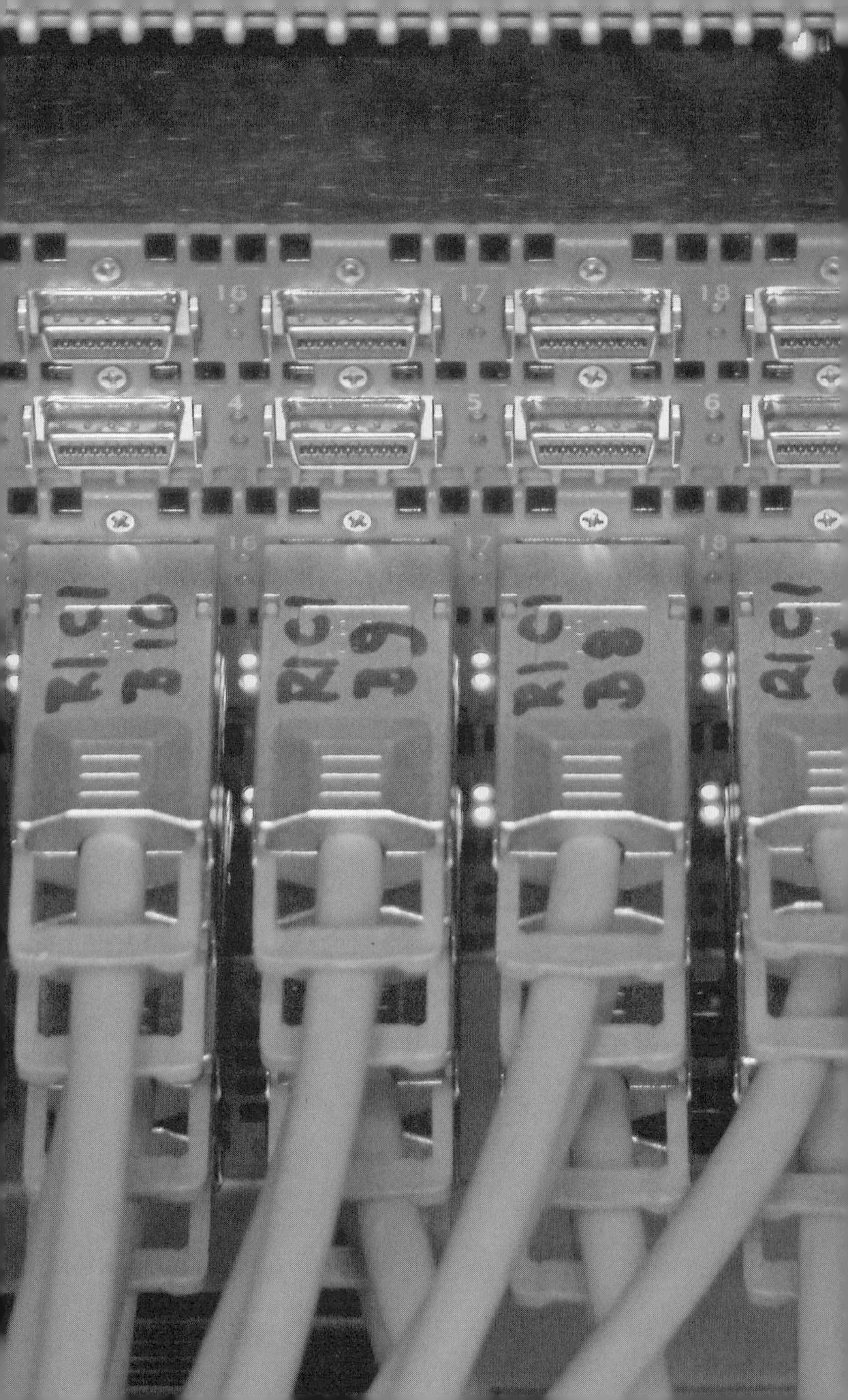
16
17
18
4
5
6

In the Cloud

The key to Microsoft's success would soon hinge on its ability to adapt to cloud computing. This delivery system uses **servers** hosted on the Internet to store and manage data that can be accessed by users through their own personal computers. Satya Nadella, who had been working at Microsoft since 1992, would be instrumental in leading that effort.

OPPOSITE: Before wireless technologies existed, all computers were connected to the Internet or other networks through physical cables.

Nadella was leading research and development for Microsoft in 2008, when the company made its first foray into cloud computing with the introduction of Windows Azure. Azure was an Internet version of Windows. It was run through Microsoft's own data centers, rather than on an individual's personal computer.

Azure was designed to facilitate app development and to provide businesses with the space to build their computing structure in the cloud. In 2011, when Nadella took over responsibility for the company's cloud computing

TAKEAWAY

The company's first major purchase under Nadella's leadership was a Swedish game company called Mojang. Mojang was best known for a popular computer game called *Minecraft*.

segment, the company released Office 365 on the cloud. Suddenly, users could access their email and other files from any computer or device and use the Office suite of programs from anywhere.

Steve Ballmer retired in 2014 after 34 years with Microsoft. Bill Gates stepped down as chairman of the board that same year. Nadella was promoted to CEO—only the third person to hold that title in

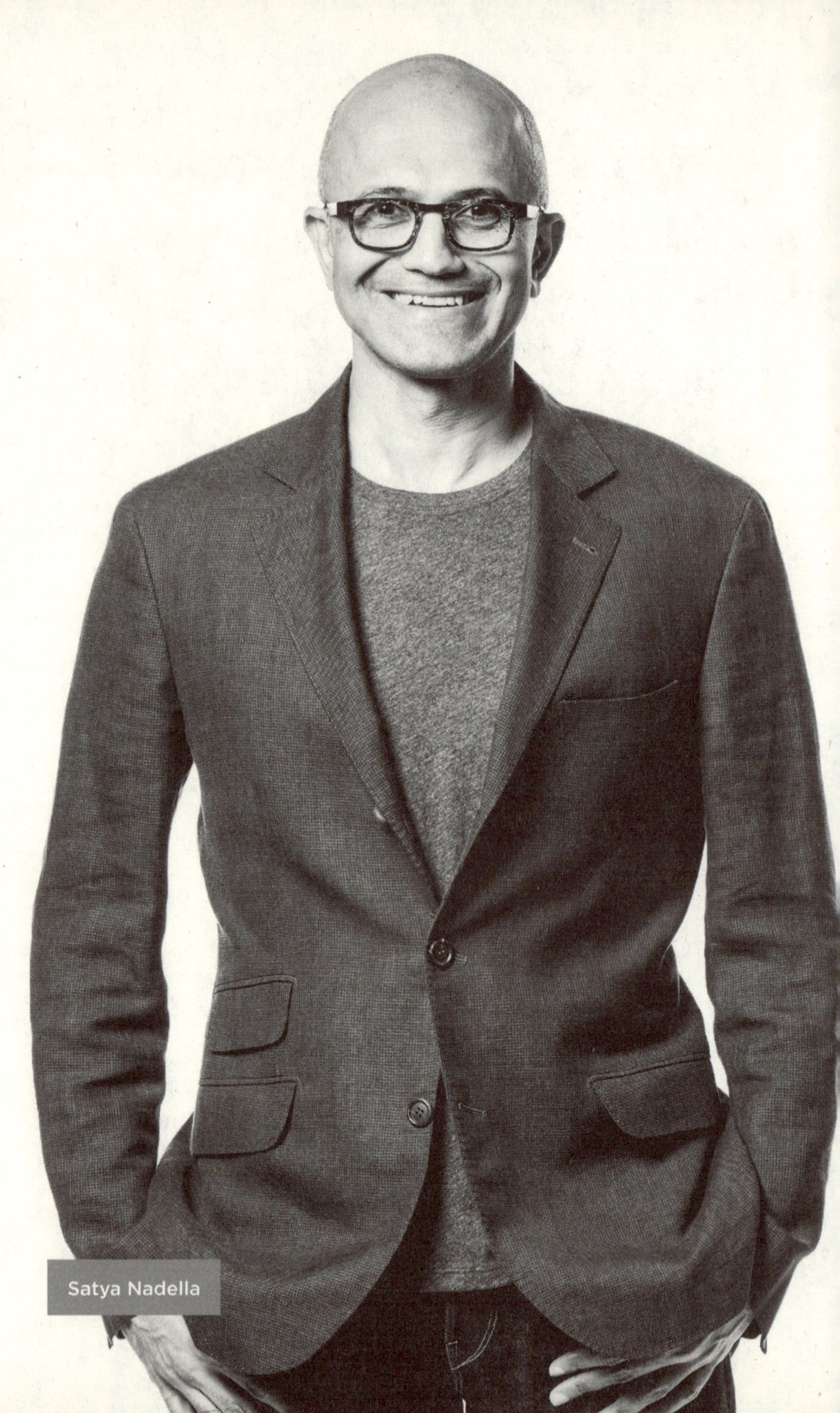

Satya Nadella

company history. He immediately put a priority on enhancing Microsoft's presence in cloud computing. He also tried to shift the culture at the company, which had grown more negative over time. "People would walk around our campus thinking we are God's gift to mankind," Nadella said. "Whether it's in ancient Greece or modern Silicon Valley, there's only one thing that brought companies, societies, and civilizations down—hubris [excessive pride]."

Nadella's humble approach to leadership helped reset expectations at Microsoft. He brought a new focus on collaboration, openness, and innovation that revived both the company's culture and its profits. Under Nadella, Microsoft shed ventures that weren't successful, including its effort to enter the smartphone market by buying Finnish phone maker Nokia. It also made several key **acquisitions** to get back on track.

The company's first major purchase under Nadella's leadership was a Swedish game company called Mojang. Mojang was best known for a popular computer game called *Minecraft*. In the game, players explore a 3D world and build their own worlds out of blocks. Microsoft made

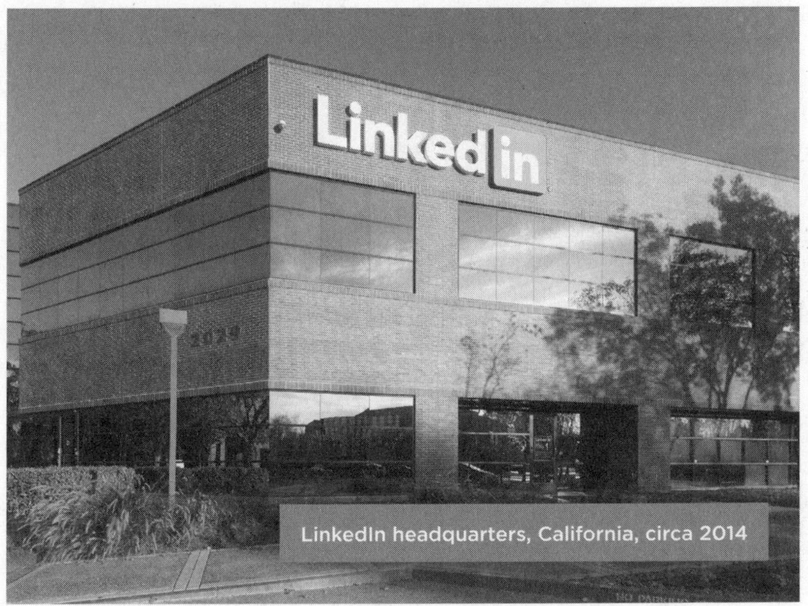

LinkedIn headquarters, California, circa 2014

Minecraft available for its own Xbox and other gaming platforms, too. It also created an educational version of the game that included lesson plans related to coding, history, geography, and math.

In 2016, Microsoft paid more than $26 billion for professional social networking site LinkedIn. It was the largest acquisition in company history and Microsoft's first venture into social media.

The primary goal was to help LinkedIn grow. Microsoft also wanted to create new opportunities for its software, including Office 365.

Within three years, LinkedIn's user base increased by almost 50 percent—from about 433 million users to more than 645 million users. "Things have certainly exceeded our expectations," said LinkedIn CEO Jeff Weiner, who stayed with the site under Microsoft's ownership. "We had a pretty aggressive plan in place, and we've been able to outperform that plan."

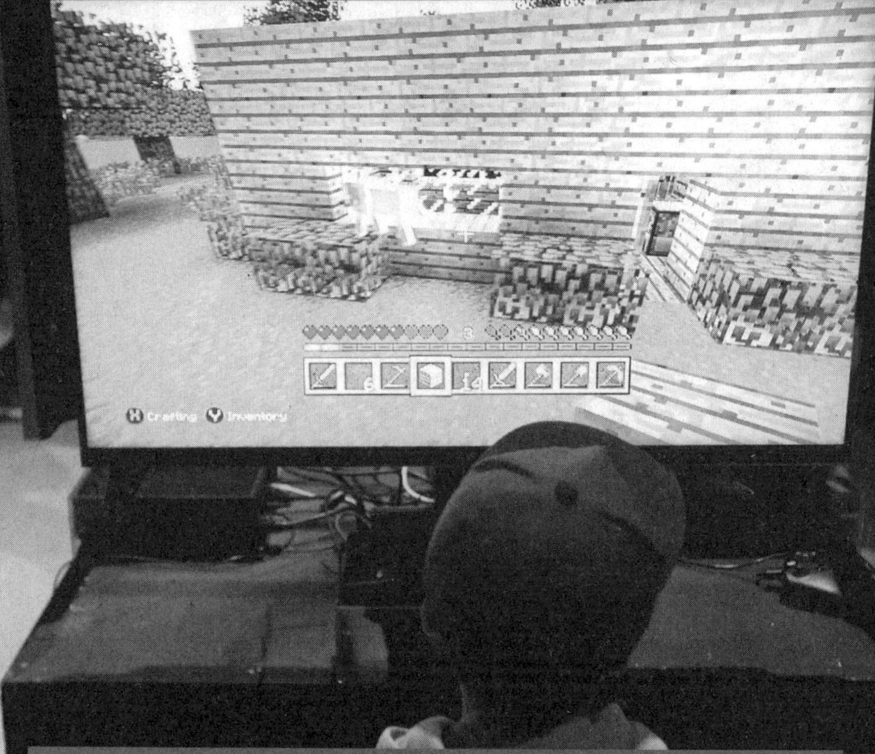

Virtual Headquarters

Microsoft used the game *Minecraft* to give its employees a look at the updates planned for its headquarters in Redmond, Washington. Designers from Blockworks, a company that uses *Minecraft*'s digital building blocks to create renderings of real-life plans, created a digital tour of the new buildings and exterior spaces. The digital experience was shared with employees when the updates were announced in 2017. The creation of the *Minecraft* version took only a matter of weeks. The actual renovations, however, took much longer. Although construction was originally expected to be complete within four years, as of fall 2023, the work was ongoing.

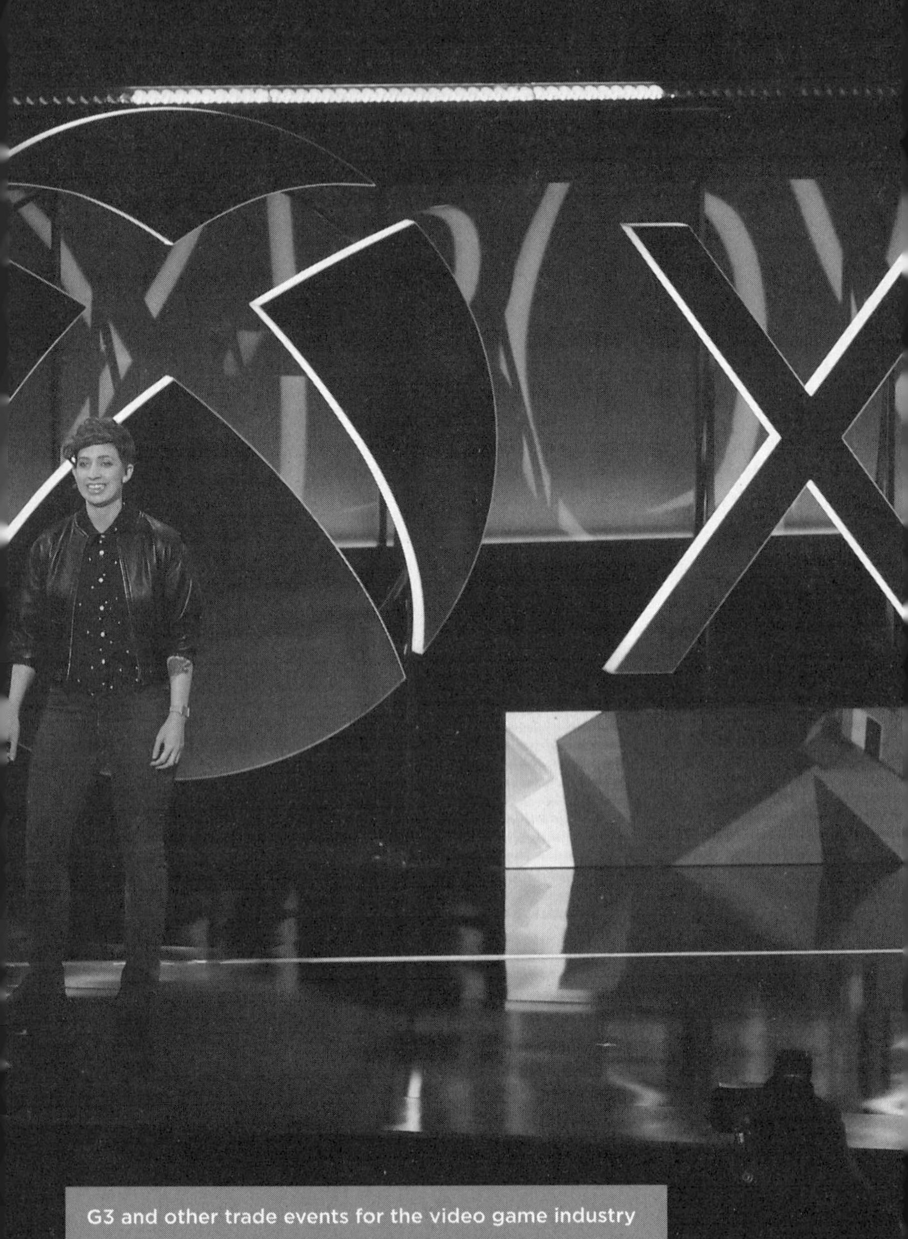

G3 and other trade events for the video game industry allowed Microsoft to showcase its latest Xbox products.

BOX

Microsoft's 2017 expansion boom extended to Milan, Italy, with the opening of new office space.

Microsoft was back on top. Its stock value was surging, and its workforce was focused on growth. In 2017, it announced major renovations to its campuses in Redmond, Washington, and Silicon Valley—a region in northern California that is home to several high-tech companies. The changes in Redmond made room for the company to hire up to 8,000 more people. It also added outdoor workspaces, treehouses, trails, and sports fields. In California, the focus was on enhancing sustainability by adding solar panels and reducing dependance on reservoirs for water.

Microsoft continued to build on its Windows and Office enterprises, expanding the suite to include such cloud-based services as Teams and OneNote.

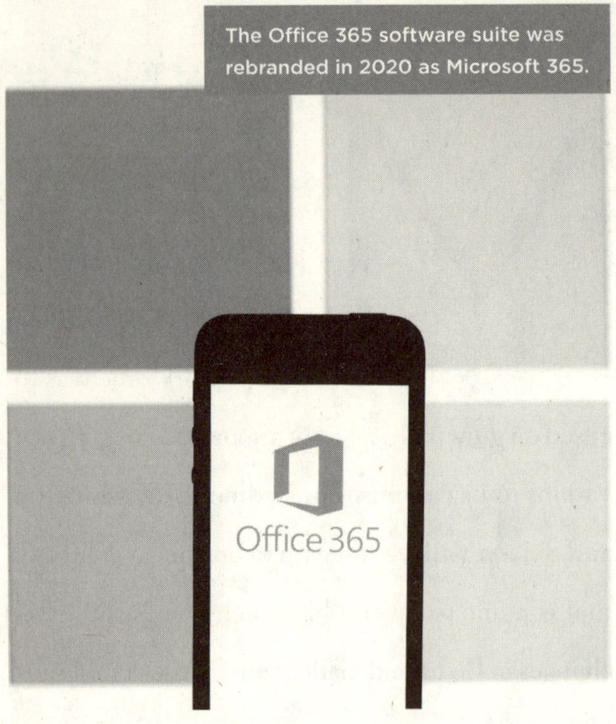

The Office 365 software suite was rebranded in 2020 as Microsoft 365.

It also continued to grow its presence as a leader in cloud computing. It expanded Azure to encompass more than 140 companies worldwide, enhancing its capabilities to better serve its customers. "We are investing aggressively to build Azure as the world's computer," Nadella said in 2018.

But Microsoft was also investing in the development of another computer. In 2020, it announced a supercomputer hosted in Azure that could build large AI models and eventually serve as a platform for other developers to work on. The supercomputer was built as a partnership with OpenAI, which would bring ChatGPT and other AI advancements to the public in 2023. Microsoft, meanwhile, continued its own work in AI as part of its overall mission to "help every person and organization on the planet achieve more."

From its beginning as a BASIC software company to its work to build AI models, Microsoft has a history of innovation. As the world of technology continues to grow and change, Microsoft will grow and change with it. With almost four decades of success already behind it, the company is ready to face whatever the future has in store for it.

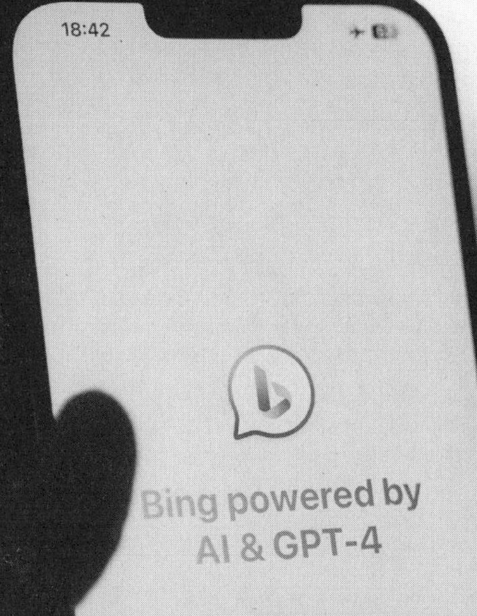

Bing Gets Better

When Microsoft introduced its search engine, Bing, in 2009, it couldn't compete with Google, which had already established itself as the world's largest search engine. But in February 2023, Microsoft got ahead of the competition. It released Bing AI, which uses AI and a new chat feature to provide better, more complete search results and the ability to create content. It can also cite its sources, which adds credibility to the service. "AI will fundamentally change every software category, starting with the largest category of all—search," said Satya Nadella, the CEO of Microsoft.

Selected Bibliography

Good, Dan. *The Microsoft Story: How the Tech Giant Rebooted Its Culture, Upgraded Its Strategy, and Found Success in the Cloud*. Nashville, Tenn.: HarperCollins Leadership, 2020.

Isaacson, Walter. "Dawn of a Revolution." *The Harvard Gazette.* September 20, 2013. https://news.harvard.edu/gazette/story/2013/09/dawn-of-a-revolution.

Microsoft.com. "About Microsoft." June 5, 2023. https://news.microsoft.com/about.

Nadella, Satya, with Greg Shaw and Jill Tracie Nichols. *Hit Refresh: The Quest to Rediscover Microsoft's Soul and Imagine a Better Future for Everyone*. New York: Harper Business, 2017.

Wallace, James, and Jim Erickson. *Hard Drive: Bill Gates and the Making of the Microsoft Empire*. New York: Wiley, 1992.

Glossary

acquisition the purchase of a company by another company

antitrust relating to laws regulating businesses to prevent unfair competition by building monopolies

appeal to apply to a higher court of law for a reversal of a decision made by a lower court

artificial intelligence the ability of computer systems to perform tasks that normally require human intelligence, such as speech recognition and decision-making

board of directors an executive committee that governs the actions of a business or organization

code program instructions for a computing system

entrepreneur a person who organizes a new business venture and assumes the risks associated with it

executive a decision-making leader of a company, such as a president or chief executive officer (CEO)

hardware computers and the associated physical equipment directly involved in processing data

innovation something that is original or advanced beyond the usual

investment a commitment of money or other resources in order to earn a financial return

marketing the process of promoting products or services

monopoly the exclusive control of the supply of a product or service

operating system a software program that manages the hardware and software resources for a computer system

philanthropic promoting the welfare of others, usually through the donation of money to causes that help people in need

profit the amount of money that a business keeps after subtracting expenses from revenues

revenue the money earned by a company; another word for income

search engine a computer program that finds and retrieves files or data from a computer network or the Internet based on search terms entered by a user

server a type of computer that accepts and responds to requests made over a network

stock shared ownership in a company by many people who buy shares, or portions, of stock, hoping the company will make a profit and the stock value will increase

Websites

Bill Gates
https://www.biography.com/business-leaders/bill-gates
Discover how Bill Gates became one of the richest men in the world.

Business
https://www.timeforkids.com/g56/sections/business
Read about successful businesses and the people who run them.

Microsoft
https://wiki.kidzsearch.com/wiki/Microsoft
Learn more about the history of Microsoft and the products it creates.

Index

More Titles from the Creative Companies Series

Jaico's creative companies series explores how today's great companies operate and inspires young readers to become the entrepreneurs and businessmen of tomorrow.

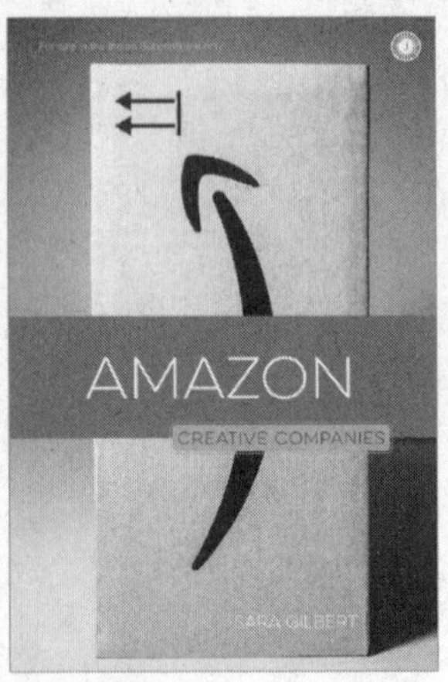

Amazon

Jeff Bezos founded Amazon in 1994 in a garage in Seattle, Washington, as an online bookstore. On July 16, 1995, Bezos launched the site, named after the vast Amazon River, and invited 300 friends to beta test it. Within 30 days, Amazon sold books across the U.S. and 45 countries, achieving meteoric success without press promotion. Today, Amazon is an e-commerce giant, offering a vast array of products and services while continuously innovating under Bezos's visionary leadership.

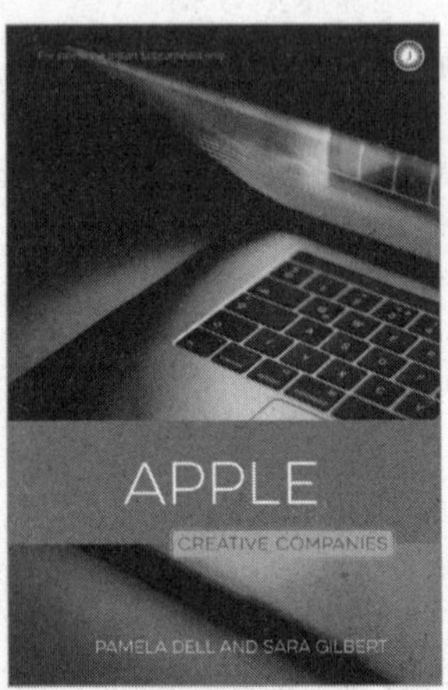

Apple

Did you know, Apple—the company behind your iPod, iPad, iPhone—began as a project shared by two ambitious boys in their computer club? When Steve Wozniak designed a computer in 1976, his friend Steve Jobs immediately saw its potential for a mass market. They found their first 'customer' at their local hobby club meeting and Apple Computer was born. Over the next 30-plus years, their company would transform the computer industry.

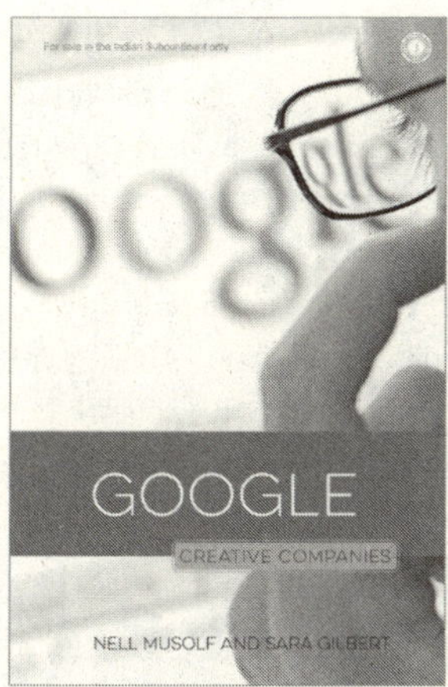

Google

This is the inspiring story of Larry Page and Sergey Brin, the founders of Google, who first met at Stanford University, in 1995. Most people would not even be aware of the fact that the very first Google office was in a friend's rented garage. Page and Brin soon began working on a likely doctoral thesis, which involved an attempt to download the complete World Wide Web, after which they would create a way to search the web, with the help of links. After many issues that involved budgeting and design, Google came into being.

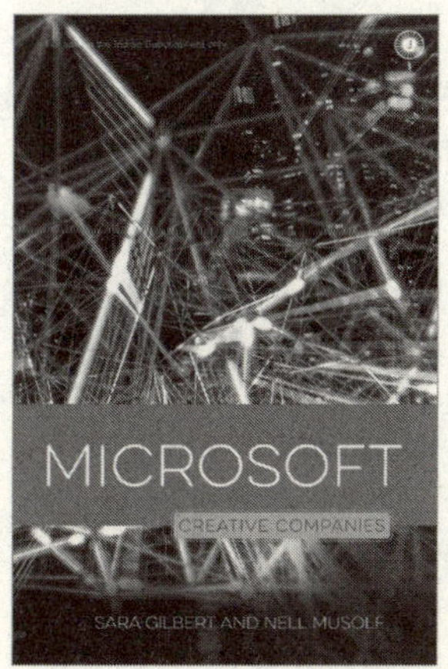

Microsoft

Bill Gates was in his second year of college at Harvard when he and his partner Paul Allen launched their own computer software company. Throughout their years at Lakeside School, Bill Gates and Paul Allen spent as much time as they could working on computers, becoming good friends in the process. Their company's impact has been such that the name 'Microsoft' has become virtually synonymous with computer software.

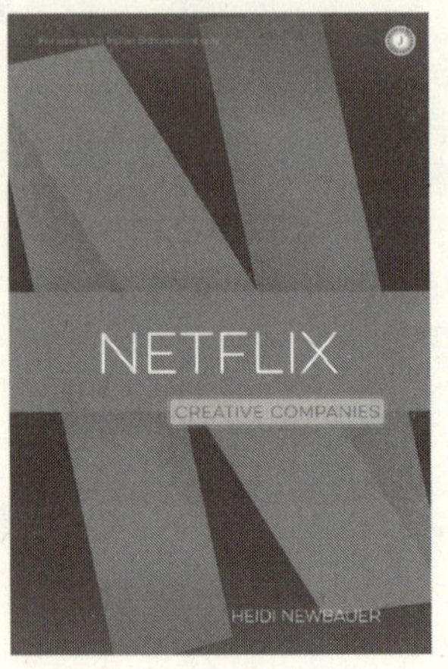

Netflix

Netflix was founded in 1997 by Reed Hastings and Marc Randolph in California as a DVD rental-by-mail service. Hastings was inspired after incurring a $40 late fee on a VHS rental, sparking the idea for a subscription-based model. In 2007, Netflix pivoted to online streaming, offering on-demand entertainment. By 2013, it expanded into original programming with hits like House of Cards. Today, Netflix is a global streaming powerhouse, revolutionizing how audiences consume movies and TV shows across the world.

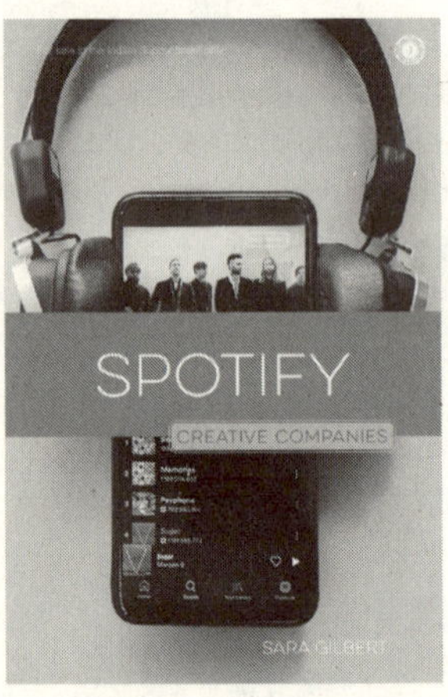

Spotify

Spotify was founded in 2006 by Daniel Ek and Martin Lorentzon in Stockholm, Sweden, as a response to music piracy. They envisioned a legal platform offering instant, affordable access to a vast music library. Launched in 2008, Spotify introduced a freemium model with ads and premium subscriptions. Its curated playlists and personalized recommendations reshaped music consumption. Today, Spotify is a global leader in audio streaming, boasting millions of tracks and podcasts, transforming how listeners discover and enjoy music worldwide..

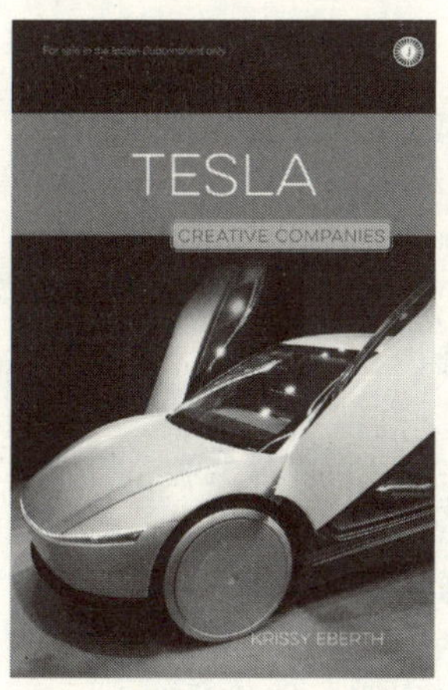

Tesla

Tesla was founded in 2003 by Martin Eberhard and Marc Tarpenning, with Elon Musk joining shortly after as an investor and chairman. Named after inventor Nikola Tesla, the company aimed to revolutionize transportation with electric vehicles. In 2008, Tesla launched the Roadster, proving EVs could be high-performance. Musk's leadership expanded Tesla's vision to sustainable energy solutions, including solar products and battery storage. Today, Tesla leads the EV industry, pushing innovation and advancements in autonomous driving.

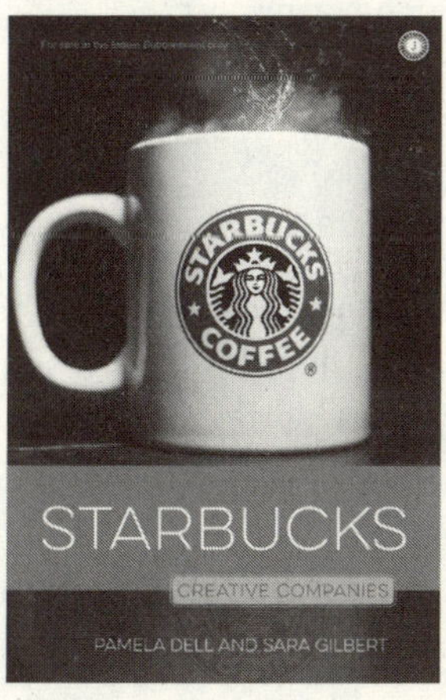

Starbucks

Starbucks was founded in 1971 by Jerry Baldwin, Zev Siegl, and Gordon Bowker in Seattle, Washington, as a single store selling high-quality coffee beans and equipment. Inspired by Italian coffee culture, Howard Schultz joined in 1982 and later transformed Starbucks into a café-centric brand, emphasizing premium coffee experiences. The first café opened in 1984, revolutionizing coffee consumption. Today, Starbucks operates thousands of locations globally.

JAICO PUBLISHING HOUSE

Elevate Your Life. Transform Your World.

ESTABLISHED IN 1946, Jaico Publishing House is home to world-transforming authors such as Robin Sharma, Sadhguru, Osho, the Dalai Lama, Deepak Chopra, Eknath Easwaran, Paramhansa Yogananda, Devdutt Pattanaik, Radhakrishnan Pillai, Morgan Housel, Napoleon Hill, John Maxwell, Brian Tracy, and Stephen Hawking.

Our late founder Mr. Jaman Shah first established Jaico as a book distribution company. Sensing that independence was around the corner, he aptly named his company Jaico ('Jai' means victory in Hindi). In order to service the significant demand for affordable books in a developing nation, Mr. Shah initiated Jaico's own publications. Jaico was India's first publisher of paperback books in the English language.

While self-help; religion and philosophy; mind, body and spirit; and business titles form the cornerstone of our non-fiction list, we publish an exciting range of current affairs, history, biography, art and architecture, travel, and popular science books as well. Our renewed focus on popular fiction is evident in our new titles by a host of fresh young talent from India and abroad.

Jaico's translations division publishes select bestselling titles in over 10 regional languages including Gujarati, Hindi, Kannada, Malayalam, Marathi, Tamil, and Telugu. These include titles from renowned national and international authors like Sudha Murthy, Gaur Gopal Das, Swami Mukundananda, Jay Shetty, Simon Sinek, Ankur Warikoo and Jeff Keller.

Visit our Website

Boasting one of India's largest book distribution networks, Jaico has its headquarters in Mumbai, with branches in Ahmedabad, Bangalore, Chennai, Delhi, Hyderabad, and Kolkata. This network ensures that our books reach all parts of the country, both urban and rural.